NO MORE US

Navigating a Divorce or Separation You Didn't Want

KRISTIN LITTLE, LMHC

No More Us: Navigating a Divorce or Separation You Didn't Want

While all of the patient stories described in this book are based on true experiences, the names given are pseudonyms. The stories are composites of similar situations with details changed for educational purposes and to protect each individual's privacy.

Cover and Interior Design by GKS Creative

ISBN: 978-1-7327160-0-1
eISBN: 978-1-7327160-1-8

Published by
Kristin Little Publishing
Seattle, Washington 98199

I dedicate this book to my family—

To Sebastian, who provides me an abundance of everyday joy I never thought possible. I am ever grateful to be your mom.

To S, for being a truly honorable man and a great dad, and for sticking with the hard work of being my parenting partner and friend.

To T, for having the courage and heart to honor what came before; for the amazing and beautiful SR; and for being a fierce and awesome mama.

To Mom, Dad, and Leslie, for teaching me that family doesn't need to be perfect—just stubbornly, lovingly committed to one another, always.

CONTENTS

Introduction

This is a book for those who have been "left." I struggled greatly in deciding on the perspective for this book due to my fear of failing to convey the difficult and complicated struggles for those who chose to end their relationships. I have great compassion for the people who made that immense decision, particularly for those who have the courage to do so with honesty and responsibility. In the end, however, I decided it was important to write deeply about what I know best rather than writing broadly about what I understand on the whole.

I also struggled with writing this book from a married woman's perspective. I am fully aware that being left is not limited to one gender or one type of committed relationship. I hope that men and those in domestic partnerships and same-sex marriages can find this book helpful, as well. However, I wanted to be able to use my voice freely and not become mired in pronouns. This is a profoundly emotional issue and I hope the men reading this book can see beyond my words to the understanding and compassion I want to convey.

My intention and greatest hope is that *No More Us* offers empathy and understanding to those who are isolated and confused by their own emotional process as they journey through a separation and/or divorce not of their choosing. I hope to support and encourage both women and men to find alternatives to the stereotypical identities others may ascribe to them, such as "angry," "vindictive," "victim," or "superwoman." Instead,

I offer a more human and flexible identity that encompasses the stronger and the weaker parts, the sadness and the hope, and the acknowledgement of the past while focusing on the future. My belief is that by doing so, we can become more resilient for ourselves, our former partners, and most important—for those who are parents—our children.

How to Use the Exercises in This Book

The exercises in this book are intended to help you develop a habit of taking some uninterrupted time for yourself each day. It might be difficult to find, but it is essential to make taking care of yourself and tending to your needs the highest priority at this time. I recommend using a journal to do the book's exercises or simply reflect and write about your experiences each day. I also encourage you to look back periodically and see how your thoughts and feelings change or solidify over time. Ask yourself whether what you anticipated happening or feeling was accurate or different than you expected.

As you move through this time of crisis, journaling can give you a way to reflect within the important context of what was happening when you made decisions, took actions, and experienced emotions. It allows you to see your growth or where you may get "stuck" and begin to know yourself more fully with compassion rather than judgment, and to grow in confidence as you keep moving forward.

Note to Readers

This book is divided into two parts. Part One addresses what often begins as a private and emotional journey as you are forced to consider the possibility of your relationship ending. Of course, not everyone has the same experience, but I do my best to follow the process as it commonly unfolds over time from private to more public changes—beginning with the disorienting shock and disbelief to grappling with how to share the news with others.

In Part Two, these emotional experiences are organized according to the more overt changes in family relationships and structure and the tasks associated with each stage—from separation to establishing a two-home family if you have children. My goal is to offer guidance and support while capturing how you might be feeling and thinking as you enter, move through, and emerge from each stage of change.

PART ONE

Falling to Pieces: Making It Through the Breakup

CHAPTER 1

The Unwelcome Welcome to the Club

THE REALIZATION THAT your marriage is ending may come as a slow, anguished awakening or in a searing flash of recognition. You may slowly shift out of denying the terrible reality that you desperately wanted to avoid. Or you might be forever changed by a few words that cannot be unsaid. You may sense a shift, either in pieces or all at once, from the world before to the world that begins now—the world without an "us." What to do with all the pain, sorrow, anger, and fear, and with all the dreams that have been suddenly taken from us?

My journey into the world of divorce began with words, both unexpected and devastating. It was as if a wave of awful comprehension pulled everything from me. I saw the colors of the rug I knelt on and the sun in the trees outside, and I thought of my one-year-old son sleeping peacefully upstairs as our world tumbled apart. Although I wanted to stay and fight, plead, beg—I knew that for the first time in my marriage, whatever I said or did would not move my husband. The tether that bound us together no longer connected me to him, and I could not bear to see the evidence that he was indeed gone. In those moments of silence, I suddenly felt exposed and did not want to grant my husband the intimacy of seeing me fall apart. So I left and, hesitantly, called my sister, feeling pulled between heaving my sorrow onto those closest to me and not wanting to worry anyone needlessly.

This can't be true, I thought. He would change his mind; he was depressed, and this was my wake-up call. Maybe it was that new medication he was taking. Maybe it was the beautiful new woman at his office. I would get another chance to make this right. We would fight and I would do whatever it took to make this better. We would be okay.

However, upon my return there were no tears or recanting—only sadness and fear in my husband's eyes. There was no fight, no second chances, only finding solace in keeping to our daily routine and trying to pretend that what was happening to us was not. We washed dishes, changed diapers, slept side by side—all while knowing that everything we knew had been forever changed.

If you are reading this book, you probably have your own "moment." My experience, the beginning of my journey, may or may not be like yours. You may have reacted similarly or drastically different. The purpose of this book is to give you some company and understanding during a very lonely time, *not* to tell you what to do. It's to help you make sense of what just happened and what is happening and maybe answer the question of why you found yourself hurling a burrito across the kitchen. (I like to think it was the therapist in me that kept me from actually aiming.) This book is about how to gain clarity about where you are, forgive yourself for maybe being a bit less than rational, and have freedom to begin to act rather than just react to what lies in your path.

So what did you do, what did you say, when your world began to shatter? Did you fight or plead, believing that expressing the depth of your anger or sadness would compel your partner to reconsider? Did you simply give rein to your feelings of betrayal and pain in order to inflict it back in equal measure? Or did you, instead, simply refuse to believe it in an attempt to make it not true? You may have stayed or you may have left with angry or sad parting words or in complete silence. You may have even tried all of the above to find anything that would work, anything that would stave off the pain or at least get a reaction—any reaction—that would connect you to the person you love. Your panic and anguish when you could not connect was not only okay, it was normal. It was called for. I hope your children, if you have them, were blissfully unaware and no one was hurt. That's about as much as anyone can expect.

So my first piece of advice is: don't let anyone tell you what you should have or could have done or shame you for being exactly as you were at that moment. I'm sure you can piece together those not-your-best moments all by yourself. You might want to get acquainted with being a little less than your totally "together" self. Superwoman with grace and poise is not in this club. You are messy, anguished, and a little bit unpredictable, and we will take you as you are—welcome.

CHAPTER 1 EXERCISES: EMOTIONAL TRIAGE

Find some uninterrupted time alone and focus your thoughts on the present and the next several days or few weeks. The purpose of this exercise is to develop a way to function in the midst of the storm by building in basic-needs self-care, as well as setting aside time free from the emotional turmoil to accomplish important tasks. You may have difficulty with some of the basics, so the following are some suggestions:

1. Make sure you are eating at least three times a day. You may need to remind yourself with an alarm or have quick, easy-to-digest meals and snacks at the ready.
2. Get enough restful sleep. A lack of sleep can make mental health issues more challenging, increase anxiety and depression, and impair your ability to think clearly. Try meditation and/or daily naps to give your body a chance to rest.

3. Exercise regularly to release stress and improve sleep. Gentle, regular exercise is recommended and getting outside is helpful to improve mood and sleep quality.
4. If you find yourself unable to establish basic eating or sleeping routines on your own, or if you are experiencing significant anxiety or depression, I encourage you to make an appointment with your doctor to discuss how to address your symptoms promptly.
5. Create a daily routine where you can set aside the emotional and focus on the practical.

   ◊ List your daily routines.

   ◊ Scan your list to identify the essential tasks and determine whether there are any nonessential tasks.

   ◊ Mark the essential tasks and consider rescheduling or omitting those that may not be priorities.

   ◊ Plan a brief period each day, as well as some longer blocks of time, to allow emotions to surface freely and safely or plan for emotional conversations with your partner. I encourage you to schedule work- and child-free time as that will likely not happen–or be frequent enough–without you actively planning for it.

   ◊ Know that there will be times when you can't contain your emotions, so learn to be kind and patient with yourself. If you find emotions and worries arise during your daily routine, acknowledge your emotions but gently and firmly remind yourself you will consider them at a later time.

   ◊ When you can, reflect on how well this strategy is working and whether some tasks/times are difficult to manage without negative emotions breaking through. Ask yourself if there is something you need during these times or, if not harmful to you or others, consider allowing yourself to be "messy" while still getting the job done.

CHAPTER 2

How Can I Fix It?

AFTER TEN YEARS together, Tammy's husband, Tom, explained he needed a "break." Tom insisted he couldn't say much more other than that he needed space from the marriage, from her, in order to figure things out after failing to get an anticipated promotion. Tammy was rational—so rational, in fact, that she consoled him, packed his things, and delivered them to his new apartment.

When Tammy came to my office, she was resolved to support her husband and her marriage vows. Her hope was that if she allowed him the freedom to seek his own answers, he would come back full of remorse for what he had done and gratitude for the space she had selflessly provided. This approach was a great fit for her: she was strong, caring, and independent, and she could take this head on with understanding and love, as she had with every other trial in her life.

At first Tom reassured her he wanted to stay in contact regularly and work on the relationship. Several awkward and painful dinners ensued, in which no discussion about what was happening to him or to the marriage took place. Instead, they spoke of superficial things, of mutual friends and work. Any attempt Tammy made to speak of her deep suffering was rebuffed. She anticipated each dinner with panic and left with a profound sadness that refused to lift. As the weeks passed, the dinners and the phone calls became fewer, and the "working on it" never materialized. She began complaining of intense panic whenever the phone rang or her coworkers asked how she and her husband spent the weekend. She was unable to sleep more than a few hours a night. After a few months, while paying bills one day, she noticed many calls to one number in particular. Tammy slowly began to realize that Tom's space was not just from her but it was space to include someone else.

Maybe you sympathize with Tammy and, like her, desired to save your marriage through love and support. Maybe you think she was naïve, and you intend to challenge your partner and make it perfectly clear the choice he or she has to make. We all need to make our own decisions that we can live with. They must fit our own values, even if our partner is not working in unison. Making this decision is the first step toward taking hold of our power—regardless of whether those attempts succeed or fail.

In my experience, one of the traits that define the women who have come through the breakup intact and healthy is the belief that they followed their own sense of what they needed rather than listening to friends or their partner or advice from a book (take note). When they were wrong, they continued to pride themselves on being authentic for what they needed at the time. They believed in their right to make decisions and make mistakes.

If You Know How I Feel, You Won't Leave

One way people try to "fix" the crisis is to appeal to their partner's empathy. It is entirely understandable to want to share your sadness and anger, to try and make them reconsider their decision—or, at least, make them share in the suffering. It makes perfect sense: this is the person with whom you have shared every high and low point, the first person you went to at the end of the day. How would you not want to share this, as well?

Unfortunately, most partners are in very different places and feeling very different things when a breakup is imminent. Both of you are suffering, even if you might not feel any sympathy for your partner right now—that is for later, much later, if ever. They may have been giving the decision to leave months of thought, slowly processing the reality that has so suddenly been thrust upon you. They may be miles down the road from the initial panic and deep grief that you now feel. Although your desire is valid—you deserve to be heard, be felt, and receive comfort—the distance between you and them often makes connection and empathy almost impossible.

Trying to Change Their Minds

Expecting your partner to reconsider, given your suffering, is also normal. In the past, when you expressed pain, your partner usually responded in an attempt to ease your suffering. It is difficult to grasp that the things that held you together, the emotional contract, has changed. They may no longer feel tied to you in the same way. They may no longer feel responsible for helping you to feel better and respond in the same way when you are suffering.

They may no longer have the same motivation to reconnect or comfort you in order to put the relationship back into equilibrium, or they may fight that familiar instinct to force the change they feel needs to happen. Whatever their reasons, they are trying to change or end the relationship. Trying to get them to take it all back will most likely be met with resistance. Yes, there is the possibility they could recant, but, at this point, it would most likely be a reaction from guilt or to make the pain go away.

I Don't Believe You

The alternate approach—denying the truth of your partner's disclosure—can arise from hoping that your commitment, alone, can sustain you both through this dark period. You plan, wait, and love from a distance, respecting your partner's autonomy by allowing them to examine whether their unhappiness can be relieved in another, far less devastating way. There are a lot of messages in our culture about love, commitment, and sacrifice that support taking this path. And for some people that strategy can be successful. I can only be impressed with the strength it takes to love while feeling anguish and maintain trust when there is no reason to feel secure. I am, without any irony, envious of those happy endings.

If you choose this path, I applaud you. However, at the outset, you may not fully understand how difficult it is to commit yourself to sustaining the loving partner role in the face of your partner's emotional and often physical absence. It can be a costly decision to put aside your own needs and fears without any assurances that your partner will return. You may hold yourself to unrealistic expectations of compassion, patience, and a sense of control. These expectations may lead you to feel you have "failed" when the inevitable outburst of emotion happens or when it isn't working according to plan. You may bury your valid feelings of anger and rejection, sadness and resentment, and ultimately hold yourself inappropriately responsible for your partner's behavior and the success or the failure of your marriage. Yet only you know what you can bear.

CHAPTER 2 EXERCISES: EXPLORING YOUR GRIEF PROCESS

Ask yourself what emotions you are feeling in the beginning of this process. Make a list of those that come to mind and answer the following questions:

1. Are some emotions more dominant or frequent than others? What are they?
2. Which emotions do you have difficulty feeling or tend to avoid feeling?
3. If there are feelings that are difficult or you are avoiding, how might you plan for supporting yourself to explore those feelings safely?

4. Are there some emotions you feel at certain times or are triggered by certain events? If so, write about the event/situation and note the emotion it elicits with an arrow. If there is a behavior that tends to follow the emotional trigger, note the behavior the emotion elicits with an arrow.

   (e.g., After kids go to bed → Sorrow → Crying/feeling hopeless)

5. The #4 answers are a list of your "emotional triggers." You likely won't be able to change your emotions, but what, if anything, would you like to change about how you react or take care of yourself while feeling this way?

6. List some ideas of how you could make these changes and care for yourself proactively in times of vulnerability. For example, would you need something/someone during those times, an alternate plan of action, another way to cope or soothe yourself, a supportive idea, or statement to remember?

Keep this list handy and feel free to add to it as you grow in awareness of your emotions and reactions and as you begin to experience emerging emotions in your grief process.

CHAPTER 3

First Steps to Taking Care of Yourself

IT MAKES SENSE TO focus on the source of the threat to your relationship: the partner who is threatening to leave. All your instincts are metaphorically to bar their way and keep them present, listening, and engaged in the struggle. Yet you are undergoing a crisis, as well, and need to stay present, stay engaged, and listen to what is happening to you. When clients make their way to my office, the focus is almost invariably on their partner and how to keep them from leaving. Their only self-exploration tends to be about their shame, guilt, and how they may have failed or are failing in their attempts to manage the relationship. The following are ways to recognize some common self-destructive pitfalls that will needlessly consume your precious time and energy.

Dealing with Self-Criticism and Doubt

People often judge their initial reactions harshly and feel shame at being irrational or overly emotional. For people who are usually rational, competent, and in control, losing it can be a deep source of shame. This is rarely a time of grace, and holding yourself to that standard can cause needless suffering. I, for one, am quite proud—not of my actions, but that I was myself in all my crazy glory and yet did not break anything. (Okay, I broke one thing, but it was an anniversary memento, and it deserved to be broken.) I didn't hurt anyone physically (again, the burrito was not aimed), fight in front of my child, get arrested, develop an addiction, or ruin my or anyone else's professional or personal reputation. I call that success.

Maybe you think that if you had only done something differently (e.g., said too much or not enough, tried the stronger approach, or been more loving), you would still be together. This is when you need to dissuade yourself from the belief that you can control anyone else. No one is that powerful, and you are not responsible for your partner's response. They most likely had one purpose: to say the hard thing as quickly as possible. Most likely, they were not weighing their decision on how you might respond. It is to be hoped that you will have plenty of opportunities to talk this through with your partner, say what you need, and express yourself clearly. If you don't get to, then that shows how little influence you had over their actions in the first place.

Focusing Only on Fixing the Relationship

Trying to "fix" the relationship may lead you to focus all your energy on the other person and miss your own very significant experience. You may bury your anger, sadness, and grief and forget that you, too, are human and need attention and care. By caring for the relationship, you may drain yourself of the strength to also care for yourself. Remember that you want to come through this whole, regardless whether the relationship ends or succeeds, so it's a good idea to find a balance that includes recognizing and meeting your own feelings and needs.

It may be hard to ask your partner for anything during this time. You might fear they will be pushed to the edge by any requests from you. You may think negotiating in any way is somehow "going along" with the decision to end the relationship. You can make your position clear (as I'm sure you have—still, say it again if you need to).

Yet knowing what you need and making reasonable requests is an act of strength, and it can help you create some respect and boundaries that support your ability to cope. It's up to you if you feel comfortable asking, but at least take a look and try to identify what you need—even if you choose not to verbalize it.

Be prepared for your partner to have needs, as well, especially if you have children. If that is the case, this is one place where, if the request is reasonable and helpful for the kids, that you find a temporary place to stow the rage and give your partner's requests some consideration. I'll talk more about children in later sections, but, first, let's focus on you.

Getting Too Comfortable with Being the Victim

Everyone is wondering how you will weather this situation. They will be looking for signs of stress and/or treating you gingerly, as if you were fragile or some sort of unstable explosive they don't want to jostle. They may be watching carefully and hoping for signs you're "handling it" well. You yourself may feel guilty when you aren't managing this as gracefully as you would like and wonder when (or if) you are ever going to be okay again.

In the beginning, when the hurt is new and raw, there can be some protection in the anger and sadness you're probably feeling and some good reasons not to rush through this process. This isn't about "getting over" it, but you will get through it. How you move through and at what pace is really yours to decide.

For me, I now know how important it was to wrap myself in the cocoon of being the "good guy" while my ex, maybe unwillingly, took the role of the "bad guy." In that protected place of victimhood, I was able to let go of control and accept the end of the life I had known—not in a wise way, I admit—but in my own way, nonetheless. When I got mad, I got mad; when I was sad, I cried; when I felt reckless, I acted on many of my impulses (more about that crazy time later).

After a while I began to feel the constraint of being the wounded one. There was no room for anything but the drama of the latest hurt.

I was the ever-suffering star of my own sad story, listening to myself talk about how my husband could be so cruel, so unfair, and so wrong. Even in the telling, some part of me knew my soon-to-be-ex wasn't a bad person. I didn't agree with what he was doing, but he was behaving in large part responsibly and with some sensitivity to what I was going through. I also still liked many parts of him. And although I missed those parts, I was glad my son would get to enjoy them in his father. I realized that, as comfortable as the role of victim was, I did not wish to define my life and my child's life by feeling betrayed. I wanted to be happy again, and, as comfortable as my little cave of pity was, my future was elsewhere.

One of the interesting things with children is that in times of stress, they commonly regress to earlier stages of development. If they were potty trained, they may begin to wet the bed. Or a younger child may begin to suck their thumb after giving it up months earlier. Just like children, we all want to go back, travel into the past where things seemed simpler and more secure. Victimhood is just that—it's your warm cozy; you're letting someone else take the lead, giving in, and allowing yourself to float instead of flailing helplessly. It can feel mighty comforting, but eventually you are going to have to gather your strength and begin again.

I suggest that if you find yourself in the role of victim, resist any attempts to wrest yourself (or others' attempts to pry you) out of your own cave of sorrow too soon. Simply ask yourself if that truly is something you need right now. Then ask yourself again in a month and again in another month. Warn your friends and your ex; take responsibility for your stance, and reassure them that you will come out when you are good and ready.

But if you find yourself making a permanent home there, maybe it's time to reconsider what victimhood is offering you—and if you have children, how it is affecting them and your family. Your partner may hold the blame, but you're maintaining the powerlessness. I do understand what it is to lose the dreams and family you once had, but only in moving forward will you begin to feel a new self and family emerge. In victimhood there is little future, but you do have a future, and you should have a hand in its creation.

Trying to Get Over Instead of Going Through

Cali entered my office as if she were attending a business meeting. She had a large file of papers and pulled out a legal pad to take notes. She wanted to get down to business. She informed me that she although she worried about the children, she would be fine—she had gotten through worse. What she wanted from me, she asserted, was information. After a twenty-year relationship, in which she had supported her partner through joblessness and addiction, he'd ended it with his newfound sobriety.

I asked her if she was angry, to which she responded, "Feeling anger is not going to get me where I need to be. He made his decision, and I have to accept it." She assured me, "I intend to be rational. I'm not going to punish him; I just want to know how to help my kids." You may be a person, like Cali, who meets each challenge with fearless bravado: positive, strong, and courageous—people come to you for help and not the other way around. If you can change something negative, then you do, and if you can't, then you make the best of it and move on. But this is not one of those times.

You will need the support of those who care about you. And if you aren't comfortable asking for help, you might want to get comfortable, because this is not the time to go it alone. Cali's approach was admirable, but rather than rushing ahead, we explored how she would feel in the long term, living daily with the agreements she was making, without first addressing her own feelings and needs. Although she might make decisions quickly, down the road there were possible triggers that might spark feelings of anger or resentment and lead to the conflict she was attempting to avoid.

Also, was she missing an important step in finally beginning to feel heard and empowered? Maybe she could not save her relationship, but she could work to create a self-identity and new role as parent that could address her feeling less than respected in her marriage. Over time, Cali began to recognize that acknowledging her underlying feelings of betrayal and sadness and fears about the future wasn't about retribution or punishment but an important step in her personal growth and building a foundation to parent effectively with her soon-to-be ex.

Feeling is essential to healing, but it is also important to experience the full spectrum of feeling, even those that are unexpected, uncomfortable, or new. The ending of a relationship is not just about sadness; it's also about fear, longing, anger, doubt, love, rage, loneliness, guilt, and countless other feelings. They may blend or be sharply experienced as all-consuming and separate. They may feel strong or subtle, visit you unexpectedly, or be familiar companions that are wearing out their welcome.

Yet there should be some ebb and flow of a variety of emotions over time. If you find yourself feeling only one thing for a long time, it might mean you are "stuck" or do not fully acknowledge the breadth of your experience. Feeling only anger may be protecting the deeper, softer, more vulnerable feelings beneath, such as sadness or loneliness. You may not be ready to acknowledge those less intense emotions, as anger feels a lot more powerful, but they are likely there.

Remember, though, that if you feel only longing and love, you may be holding on to an unrealistic hope for reconciliation that keeps the sadness and anger at a comfortable distance. If you only feel sadness, you may be dealing by "not dealing" and finding solace in letting the unfair world move on without you. You may have never felt these things before or felt them so intensely, but they are all a part of the process. In order to get through this time, you actually have to participate fully. Although the feelings are often unwelcome, they all have important information and lessons to offer as you move through your grief.

CHAPTER 3 EXERCISES: WHAT DO ***YOU*** NEED?

Take some time to think about you. As you write the answers to the following questions, try to keep the focus on yourself and separate from whatever concerns you have about your partner's reaction or how it may affect your approach to maintaining the relationship. You are free to communicate (or not) these needs to your partner, but the important thing is first gaining some clarity about what you really need as you go forward:

1. What do you need from your ex-partner right now in order to better manage your emotions?
2. Is there anything he or she could refrain from doing or saying because it is making it harder for you?
3. What type of coordination would be helpful to manage the day-to-day duties better?
4. Do you need some time for yourself or a break from children, if you have them?
5. Is there a certain amount of contact or space that you need from your partner at this time?
6. Would some temporary ground rules help you feel less anxious?
7. How/when can you communicate about meeting your daily needs or those of your children? (Yes, if you have children you'll need to do this; their needs don't go on hold even though the two of you are in conflict.)

CHAPTER 4

But Do They Really Mean It?

WHEN I WAS A CHILD, I always hated that scene in the movies where the tamed animal was set free into the wilderness by its human companion who forced it out by cruel words and threatening gestures. The human's sadness was masked by his anger, and the animal seemed so disoriented by the cruel severing of their bond. The experience of ending a long-term relationship has some similarities. Two people are crushed by different emotions and unable to help each other because of their own needs and suffering.

You may not realize it, but you most likely do not have a full or even tentative grasp of what your partner is truly experiencing. Their feelings may prevent them from responding to you with the caring and compassion you expect; they may even respond to you with coldness or anger. Understand that, unlike in the past, your partner may not be the safest or most reliable person to console you or understand your pain. It's devastating and disorienting, I know. Let's hope a time will come when discussions can be more transparent and honest, but for now, know that your partner is experiencing something very different. You may need to wait to find your validation and compassion or learn to find it in yourself.

There may even be a desire not to believe your partner because they are acting and speaking so differently. Perhaps you think they don't mean what they are saying, and it is up to you to decipher their hidden code somehow. There is always the exception, but when someone is saying something so significant, so potentially destructive, they have probably already given it a good deal of thought.

They may have some indecision, but they felt strongly enough to disclose their troubled feelings or their intention to leave the relationship. And even if they are ambivalent or confused, it is important to at least listen to what is going on in their mind and heart and believe it. It is the only concrete information you have, and you can drive yourself crazy by trying to interpret alternate meanings, motivations, and intentions.

Also, you can frustrate and close down the communication you desperately want if you dismiss the message out of hand. However, if things are being said that go beyond explanation and seem more about shifting the heavy burden onto you—or only for the purpose of inflicting pain—you can certainly leave or tell your partner to stop. Or if the information is useful but you've simply reached your limit of what you can bear, you can respect your need to protect yourself by asking for a break.

Yes, they could be lying. They might be outright dishonest or possibly softening their truth. The former says much more about them and their ability to confront difficult issues and take responsibility, yet the latter is not uncommon and could be used to protect you both rather than as deception. If you have a partner who is basically decent with a history of honesty, they probably don't enjoy hurting you and are looking to leave without causing you any more pain.

You Should Have Known

Hearing your partner's thoughts and feelings about wanting to end the relationship is difficult, to say the least. What can make it even more crushing is if your partner claims "you should have known." If you had no idea, you may obsess over what to believe—the reality of marriage as you knew it or this darker history that your partner describes? Are they threatening to rewrite your history and what you thought was shared knowledge, feelings, and experience? To the person being left, "you should have known" falls like a death knell of everything you thought you shared.

You think back to every special moment and wonder if they were they lying or pretending. "You should have known" may seem like an insistence to forsake your most intimate moments and drain them of their emotion and meaning. You feel untethered and ungrounded; unable to grasp your future, now you cannot even hold on to your past.

"You should have known" also sounds, to the one who's left, like blame or shame. They may insist that you should have perceived the distance, the disagreements, as the winding down, the harbinger of the end. You may lie awake at night trying to recall what you missed. Yet anyone who has been married knows that a committed relationship is made up of imperfect moments of connection, difficulties, and reconnection. Fights happen, frustrations linger, and we constantly seek to be happy with what we have and strive to perfect our relationship over the years.

Anger and frustrations are not typically signs of divorce; they are signs of the imperfect struggle for intimacy. The commitment to stay is what makes us trust and sustain ourselves when things are difficult. The truth may be that your partner knew something you didn't and thought about it long before the moment you were told. Even if there were difficulties, only they thought of the possibility of leaving.

To give them the benefit of the doubt, they may have been terrified. They may have thought their feelings would pass without you ever having to know and hoped to spare themselves (and you) a ton of pain. They may have thought a vacation or a baby or the passage of time would make things better. They may have spent months or even years struggling with their feelings—but it was their feelings, their experience, not yours. There may have been great times that made them forget for a while, that made them hope. Trying to discern which moments were "real" and which ones were "pretend" will just make you crazy. They knew, or thought they knew, and they didn't tell you. You are not a mind reader.

While not true in every case, most married people do take ending the relationship with a great measure of seriousness and suffering. Whatever the reason, the person ending the relationship most likely processed many of the feelings slowly over time, all of which are crashing down on you right now. They thought of scenarios for the future and how they could make sure the worst things did not happen; they struggled through the guilt and sadness before you ever had a clue. In fact, they may be mistaken in asserting you should have known. Still, what is the point? If it feels like they are saying you should be in agreement because the relationship was obviously so seriously flawed that the end was inevitable, ask yourself if that is what you felt/saw/thought. If no, then there is your answer.

Maybe you've lost your dreams for the future, but do you need to lose your past as well? Here's what I suggest. You have no control over what your partner feels. Your partner may not even be in the best place to judge the "truth" of the past, and no one has a perfect grasp on the truth, anyway. I say, keep your history. Hold to it and honor your experience, regardless of your partner's view. You are not asking them to share your view; you are simply respecting your own truth and allowing yourself to maintain your memories and the meaning of your shared past.

Too Much Information or Not Enough

Sara's husband left her when she was on vacation. He made excuses as to why he could not accompany her to visit her family on the other coast. In a phone call, he let her know he wanted "space." When she returned, he refused to discuss the issue and quickly moved out. Sara got no real information, just enough to distract her: he was not "happy," they didn't "fit," and he wanted "time away." The not knowing was the most difficult part for Sara.

Our first sessions were all centered on the mystery of her husband's motives, hidden clues in the history of the relationship about what she could have possibly done wrong, and whether he would come back after some "space." It took a long time for her to move away from self-blame because her partner didn't give her the gift of taking responsibility for his actions. It was her deep source of pain to be left but without her husband respecting her enough to tell her why.

On the other hand, too much information can also be needlessly hurtful. When Karen came into my office, she was distraught and barely able to contain the rage she felt toward her partner, Joanne. Two days earlier, Joanne had told her that not only did she wish to leave the relationship but also that she was in love. Joanne, it seems, was in the throes of a new relationship, and in her attempt to explain to her partner the reasons behind her decision, she detailed the unexpected serendipity of a connection that was so deep, she was overpowered.

This, of course, was not helpful, enlightening, or considerate to Karen in any way. In fact, Karen's anger was so great that it overpowered every other feeling. She was unable to connect with her sadness and grief and was initially unable to contain her contempt enough to protect their children from the conflict. Although I have no idea what motivated her partner to share all of this information, I can offer a helpful ground rule to those ending their marriage: resist the temptation to expound on the wonders of their new love and designate "fate" as responsible rather than the fact that it was a decision. This is a case in which an "information overload" message from the receiving partner (or a flying burrito) might be justifiable.

Affairs, emotional or otherwise, are probably something most people won't readily admit. And if they do, it can be more about shedding their guilt or due to a lack of sensitivity than actually wanting to be honest and helpful. After seeing many partners struggle, I have come to the conclusion that it is helpful to the one being left to have some information to begin trying to piece together what happened rather than being completely in the dark.

CHAPTER 4 EXERCISES: VALIDATING YOUR OWN EXPERIENCE

Think for a moment about the reasons your partner gave for what was wrong in the relationship and why he or she wanted to end it. Close your eyes, take three deep slow breaths while holding this in your mind and when done, complete the following:

1. Name the feelings that came to you as you considered your partner's story.
2. Looking at your feelings listed, ask yourself what you likely need in response to these feelings [e.g., anger → validation/to be heard; betrayal → justice; sadness → comfort].
3. Ask yourself whether you can expect your partner to be able to meet your needs at this time. Is that a reasonable expectation? Is your partner in a place where the request might lead to more conflict or pain?
4. For each need you described, ask yourself what you most need to hear and write it down. Might you be able to give that to yourself?

Remind yourself that it's okay not to understand your partner's truth fully—or even your own—at this time. You do not have to decide which is more real or change someone else's truth. Try to let your truth and your partner's merely exist as the understanding you each hold now for reasons you may not fully grasp. Practice patience and remind yourself that you will know more as you continue on this journey; full understanding will likely come naturally in its own time. Come back to this idea and practice validating and comforting yourself when your partner cannot.

CHAPTER 5

Trying to Piece Together the "Truth"

THE NEXT QUESTION AFTER "How do I fix this?" is usually "What happened?" You're desperately seeking some understanding and a reason. My former husband and I used to have an inside joke: "I'll know you're an alien if…" whereby we could tell whether an alien had invaded the other's body, such as if I turned down any offer of dessert or if he hung up his own shirts. I actually considered this idea for a time, as it seemed as plausible an explanation as any for his departure.

I was convinced something must have profoundly altered my husband and that somehow explained the lack of familiarity and intimacy between us. You may, like I did, believe the change was due to an outside influence, such as another person or something being "wrong" with your partner, such as depression. You may decide that he or she must be a narcissist without empathy or feeling, and you simply failed to see it until now. Or possibly your search veered into self-blame: perhaps you didn't give them enough support, sex, or love. You may wonder if it was because of the weight or the wrinkles or you were too demanding/boring/critical/needy.

You might even find yourself spending hours Googling "midlife crisis" or "personality disorders," or searching through emails and text histories, or feeling tempted to call a friend with an unremarkable car to make some stealthy late-night drives around town. What is happening to you? You were probably never the jealous type before, but now you are an unrecognizable borderline stalker. The idea of a private investigator might even sound really tempting, if you had the money and you wouldn't get caught. Relax: you aren't crazy (or at least I don't think you are). It's not crazy to try to make sense of what happened; it's a basic human instinct to find reason, clarity, and understanding in dangerous situations. That's what keeps our clever species alive.

Which is not to say you should indulge those stalking fantasies, though. You may be feeling vulnerable, but doing things that go against your values might lead only to unwarranted self-criticism and even shame. It might also undermine your strength and self-compassion, both of which are basic necessities in your journey through this difficult terrain. If you are putting all your energy into trailing someone else's truth rather than looking for your own path and truth, you are much more likely to become hopelessly lost and exhausted.

Yes, you might find something, but will it truly be what you are looking for? Only you, in time, and your partner (if he someday offers you insight) will actually give you a glimmer of what happened. But you each will still have your own nuanced understanding of the situation. That kind of insight is, most likely, a long way down the road; right now it is enough to make an effort to focus on yourself and put one foot in front of the other instead of trying to understand exactly what led you to this lonely place.

Trying to figure out exactly what happened seems like a way to fix it. *If I can find out why, then maybe I can solve the problem and this will all go away.* Or perhaps you need someone other than your partner on whom to focus your anger . . . or for something to use as a weapon to inflict emotional pain that connects with or gets a response from your indifferent partner—even if the response is guilt and not love. The desire is normal, but this type of searching is counterproductive; it often hurts and becomes busy work for an unsettled, anxious heart.

Searching for Something Wrong with Your Partner

Many of my clients come in with the conviction that their partner must be depressed, which is the reason he or she is leaving. They cite the partner's lack of initiative in being part of the family, their isolation. They might refer to a difficulty with the partner's work or personal life, such as a recent death or illness of a close family member. It is true that significant negative life events can lead to an onset of anxiety or depression, and it is not a bad idea to explore that possibility directly with a person exhibiting symptoms of a mood disorder.

However, you should be prepared to consider that choosing to end a relationship is also a significantly distressing life event, and the changes you see may reflect a person deeply affected by their decision to end the marriage. They may be sad, but sad because they are leaving you. They may be anxious, but it may be because they fear the changes they know will come from their decision to leave. I know this is difficult to accept, but it is a possibility and something you should consider.

A midlife crisis is also a common theory that disoriented and anguished partners can use to explain their partner's erratic behavior. Trivializing such a significant life shift as a midlife crisis is generally a mistake, though. Yes, you might witness impulsive behaviors—some of them silly to observers—but the motivations behind them may run deeper than a yearning for youth or a desire for a new car. Many of us have or will come to a time in our lives when we take stock of how we are living and whether it satisfies or leaves us wanting.

Often, this does not come with a desire to leave our relationships. Many people take up exercise, follow an inclination to travel, or find new interests that expand their lives to fill up the empty spaces. For those who have difficulty with intimacy, acknowledging and communicating feelings, or directly addressing conflict, the urge to leave and start anew may be tempting. Leaving means no longer having to wrestle with a difficult relationship, work through resentments, and take responsibility for how they added to the hurt and misunderstandings. That would take work and courage. Some people have little experience or no role models to guide them or lack the desire to do the hard work that long-term, satisfying relationships demand.

An unwelcome truth is that for some, a time comes when they discover their relationships no longer satisfy them. They may struggle with their dissatisfaction for quite a while before deciding they do not wish to work on the relationship. Each of us must decide to be in the relationship or leave it. It is often difficult for the person who was left to know if their partner's action was born from a desire to "cut and run" or the result of a deep, slow, honest revelation.

Only time and your partner's willingness to share—along with your willingness to listen—will give you a better understanding of his or her inner experience. And maybe it doesn't really matter in the short run, but in the long run, it might make things easier to know that they acknowledged the cost of their decision at the time. However, in the initial wake of devastation, you may not care or have the energy to decipher why they are leaving.

Of course, you don't have to agree with their decision. Your values about the importance of commitment and work in a relationship and honoring vows may be a solid argument against leaving a marriage. However, as unfair as it is, as morally right as your belief in marriage is, as hurtful or wrong as you believe the decision to leave may be, the fact remains that they get to make this decision with or without your agreement.

When you have been left, it may seem paramount that your former partner validates your pain through acknowledgement or apology. However understandable the impulse, seeking retribution often leads down a very dark road, usually not anywhere you would actually choose if you were thinking clearly. Think about where you want to be, imagine yourself at peace somehow, and begin to build a life worthy of you. Remember, your healing is not dependent upon your partner's acceptance, agreement, or—at the other end of the spectrum—their suffering.

Searching for the "Other"

Another avenue of intense speculation is the search for someone else, someone new who crashed your once-stable relationship and made it careen out of control. The reason this may be a popular focus is that it is sometimes true. People do have affairs, and they often happen as a marriage begins to unravel. You may become obsessed with knowing in detail the nature of the betrayal: all the sordid details of who this person is, when the affair began, the nature of their relationship, what they did and when. You may feel duped and horribly stunned by how deeply you were disrespected by your partner's actions. You may look at all his friends and wonder who knew and participated in your suffering by not telling you. For you, the world becomes a less predictable and less trusting place.

You may, instead or additionally, turn the full force of your anger on your partner. You might want them to suffer the consequences of their actions, for everyone to know what your partner is capable of, and shame those who may have supported his behavior. This is rage; it is indeed powerful, but it is also temporary and cannot be a foundation on which you can move forward and heal. It has the power to destroy reputations, important relationships, and your own sense of dignity and self-control.

If you learn another person was involved, I'm not suggesting that you repress your anger or even rage. However, I do urge you to realize the limits of what those feelings can actually do for you in the long run and consider the destruction they can wield in the short run if you allow them to guide your behaviors. I urge you to question what it means to know that your partner was unfaithful and whether it truly has any bearing on your path to becoming whole again. It matters, yes, but in what ways and how does it affect your decisions or support you during your grief? What does it really say about your partner and their motives, abilities, and intentions? What does it say about you or your relationship? Those are the questions I wish to propose to you before you go too far down the road of seeking retribution or trying to find clear answers about your relationship from someone you may not even know.

If another person was involved, it is likely your partner was not secretly plotting to betray you or actively seeking to destroy your marriage. Rather, it is often the case that people, consciously or unconsciously unsatisfied in their lives or in their relationships, leave a space open for the opportunity of another relationship. Having an affair may say a lot about your partner's courage to acknowledge their own feelings and confront issues directly, honestly, respectfully. It may indicate their inability to stick with difficult issues and put fantasy above solving real-life problems. It might also say something about your partner's lack of awareness of how their actions affect others or their inability to postpone self-gratification, take responsibility for their actions, or place their needs above others.

That information should be more useful to you than comparing yourself relentlessly and without basis. I believe that basically good people still make big mistakes. Maybe you can't consider forgiveness at this point, but you can still try to admit that you don't have all the answers right now. Maybe you don't need or even want them at this point. Just consider that anything that plunges you headlong into despair might be something to avoid ruminating about during the first few months.

Searching for Something Wrong with You

Whether your partner was unfaithful or not—or even if you believe they are suffering some internal malady that has changed them—in my experience, the question often seems to be, "What is wrong with me?" What makes this question so common and yet so troubling is that we *all* have things we'd like to change about ourselves and ways in which we fall short. There may have been things your partner told you they wish you would change or possibly even gave as reasons for wanting to end the marriage. Maybe it isn't even something "wrong" but just a question of preference. Perhaps you or your partner feel you are too social or not social enough, not fit enough, not outdoorsy or well-read enough. Maybe you are too talkative or too silent or have difficulties in your career or with your extended family. Maybe you struggle with intimacy or have different values in parenting. Whatever things you wish were different or your partner finds fault with can become an easy targets for self-criticism. It can be a short hop from there to focusing the blame for the failure of the relationship squarely on you.

Times of transition can certainly provide opportunities for taking a good look at yourself and learning what you want to change. However, self-blame is a much different animal, and it's what I typically see in clients who are struggling with being left. It is one thing to tell yourself, *Yes, I would like to be more fit and active*, and quite another to blame the failure of your marriage on your inability to maintain a healthy weight. First and foremost, know that being loved does not depend on meeting specific standards, such as weight or income. There are many, many examples of happily married, not-so-fit, not-so-rich people out there—just take a look.

If you take your partner's standards as a way to gauge whether you were "worthy" of their commitment, then you will never truly understand the nature of love. Marriage is not a transaction or a cause-and-effect relationship in which each partner meets the criteria of the other in order to receive love in return. Love is relational, with one partner's actions affecting the other's; it is difficult and often inaccurate to pinpoint the beginning of the negative cycle. Did you begin to lose the desire for sex after the loss of connection, or was it the other way around? Did your criticism cause your partner to turn away, or did you begin to protest loudly because your partner became distant and less responsive? If you agree that your partner has pointed out areas you want to address, then go ahead and work toward bettering yourself. But do it for *you* and not as a way to fix the relationship or out of guilt. Successful relationships can embrace the imperfect, and many do.

Why So Negative? Don't You Believe in Happy Endings?

You may wonder whether I am being negative and discounting the possibility that there is hope. Perhaps in trying to find out what went wrong, you might find important information that can give you some clarity about what is wrong. Perhaps you may be given a chance to address a fundamental issue that leads your partner back and alters the path of your relationship. If that is your heart's desire, I hope the opportunity presents itself because I love happy endings.

I believe in the power of relationships to heal and that people can find new intimacy and closeness through difficult trials and hard work. But it's also my belief that two people need to choose freely and be fully engaged in order to make that happen. If you find yourself feeling that my advice is overly negative, that I am not allowing for the positive stories of hope and reunification, it is only due to the fact that I know reunification takes two equally committed people. Until your partner actually expresses a desire to work on your relationship and gives you clear indications about what is not working for them and how you might help, you would be trying to do the work for both of you.

Until then, you will have no assurances they even want you to make the effort in the first place. My suggestion is that instead of searching without any direction, ask for clarity, if it can be given. Express your desire to work on the relationship if they are willing, and let them know your offer is open until they hear differently. Then let it go. It is truly out of your hands.

Taking Care of Yourself

It can be difficult *not* to do something, anything in this time of crisis—perhaps even sit still. Alternatively, you might be someone who is unable to move at all and lets her mind do all the work. Either way, it's difficult not to listen to that inner voice screaming, "I have to know," or "I have to do something." I'm not suggesting that you get all Zen-like and wait, peacefully detached from all wanting. If that is you, well, then you certainly have something to teach me.

What this chapter is suggesting is that you take the focus off the person who chose to leave the relationship and put that energy to work for you. You may be thinking I'm talking about feeling your feelings—yes, I am, but there is more to it than that. You need to *do* something, as well, if you want to reclaim your energy and power. You have no control over your partner or the direction your life may take in terms of the relationship, but you can control and take care of yourself. You can begin finding space to create a future vision, whether or not your relationship survives.

Separation and divorce often transform people. We hear stories of people who are broken by their partner leaving, but just as often (and in my experience, the majority of) people find something new and vital in themselves in the wake of the turmoil. It is those people who, at some point, accept the realities and challenges of their lives and move forward to the best of their abilities. They glean insight and develop skills that serve to underscore the gifts of the experience rather than the tragedy. One client expressed it this way: "Even though I do not want this and I don't feel responsible for ending the relationship, I realize how much the relationship has changed me. I lost a lot of who I was, and I want it back."

When we take the focus off the other person, we can begin to gain clarity about what we are missing and what is not right with us. This is often difficult, as it means moving forward toward a destination we wish to avoid or at least delay. Also, the challenge might be that acknowledging *we* weren't fully satisfied with the union, either, means we were onboard with the idea of separation or divorce, when we were not. However, we can, even in times of deep sadness, make something positive out of our experience and show our ability to grow in spirit, mind, and body.

For example, my first big outing after the separation was difficult. I packed up the van, worried about leaving my young son for the entire weekend, and headed out to the coast. When I got to the water, instead of surfing, I slept. I was drained and allowed myself—for the first time since becoming a mother—to do what I needed when I needed it. The surfing was nothing spectacular, but I felt more alive than I had in a very long time. I enjoyed the water, the people, the quiet, and the freedom. I spent the time reconnecting with myself, and I discovered that she was a friend I had missed terribly.

During this time, I began to realize how disappointed I was that I had to be forced to discover myself through the trials of divorce rather than within my marriage. I realized that in my efforts to care for the relationship, I'd missed my husband's pleas to find more of my own way instead of handing him the responsibility of my life. Rather than resenting that he did not appreciate all I did for us, I should have been putting more effort into what I needed for myself as an individual. The awareness was bittersweet. My new vitality was mixed with sadness and grief for what our marriage might have been, and I frequently had to pull myself away from self-blame and regret. I finally realized that even if it were too late to save my marriage, I could find new strength and confidence, and wherever my path led, I could truly be whole again.

"Scorched-Earth" Strategy Isn't Worth It

When Tom's wife left, his stable world spun out of its careful balance. Tom's whole life was centered on duty, work, and behaving honorably. His wife's infidelity challenged everything he knew about how relationships were supposed to work. And when his wife did not visibly suffer, it challenged his beliefs about justice. He struggled to make himself heard, as if that would somehow right the world as he knew it. He railed against his wife and actively persuaded everyone else he knew to join in his judgment.

Tom could not acknowledge that underneath his anger, he was hurt and grieving. It was easier to burn with self-righteousness than to feel the slow, deep pull of sadness or acknowledge that in being vulnerable in love, he had been hurt. He clung to the "rules" of binding marriage vows, and he would not accept the fact that his wife could make her own decisions—however "wrong" he felt them to be.

His efforts to show her how "bad" she was took root in every aspect of their divorce. He fought every decision in an effort to indicate he did not condone the process. He fought for full custody of the children, despite his full-time work and lack of ability to actually fulfill the duties of a full-time parent. He fought for the house and the retirement account, justifying his actions as warranted based on his wife's decision to leave the marriage. "She made her bed and now she has to lie in it."

His "scorched-earth" strategy wounded everyone in his path: himself, his children, friends, and family. Yet it did not abate his suffering. The divorce professionals could not protect him from depleting the family's finances or assist him in making sound and reasonable decisions. His anger and grief had a very real and concrete cost, along with the emotional consequences.

In the end, the divorce settlement was in line with divorces lacking all the vitriol: The house was sold and equity shared; the kids' time was divided in a way that met their needs. The teenaged kids, who knew too much and initially suffered, pragmatically decided to ignore their parents' conflict, chalked it up to them "acting like children," and settled into a new routine rather than taking sides. Whether or not Tom acknowledged the fact, in the end his happiness was not tied to his wife's unhappiness.

In fact, his efforts to ensure his wife's unhappiness increased both his and his children's suffering.

When you find your path of self-focus veering into blame and criticism, stop where you are and ask yourself: Is this really where I want to go? Maybe consider a little detour along the same route that takes all of the focus off your partner and what they want and turns it back toward you. You may find that, yes, some aspects of yourself played a part in your relationship difficulties but remember that they were part of a much bigger picture.

You may want to make some changes, but make them for *yourself*, not just for your partner. You might consider that your partner is welcome to their opinions and preferences, but he or she does not determine whether you deserve or meet the criteria for love. There are many other opinions out there, including your own. You may ultimately learn many painful truths about yourself or your partner, but if you meet them with acceptance of human limitations and imperfections, you will no longer be traveling around in circles; you will be much farther along the path back to a stronger and more resilient you.

CHAPTER 5 EXERCISES: DOING SOMETHING FOR YOURSELF

If you want to do something, direct some of that crazy, searching energy onto yourself. To get some more clarity about what that actually means, take a moment to think about when you felt strong, happy, and most connected to yourself. Try to identify those moments in which you felt a sense of "knowing"; it could be a surge of fire in your belly or a feeling of "flow," where everything seemed to be as it should be.

1. When was that? What were you doing? Who were you with?

2. What does this tell you about how you might reconnect with previous parts of yourself or find exciting new ones? Allow yourself some fantasy and creativity and challenge any thoughts or beliefs that get in the way of your adventures. The possibilities are many: you could decide to reconnect with old friends, write, paint, surf, travel, get a massage, investigate new career paths, change your hairstyle–whatever calls to you. It may not go perfectly, but that is not the point. It is all in the trying.
3. Take a moment to write a list of ideas (without judgment or censorship) that spark a sense of "trueness" or excitement in you. Give this list several pages of room to expand as inspirations arise over time.
4. Revisit the list and add ideas as needed. Circle or underline the ones you tried that brought you joy or confidence, and cross out the ideas that weren't pleasurable or fulfilling. Think about why and gather clues about what connects you with your joy now and which ideas should be left in the past.

CHAPTER 6

How to Go Crazy Without Hurting Yourself or Anyone Else

AFTER A PARTNER LEAVES, you may suddenly find yourself with a freedom that you never expected or wanted; you may be unsure and hesitant. When that new freedom is combined with anger, sadness, and longing, it can be easy to go to extremes—to swing from paralyzed with indecision to impulsive or even reckless inclinations. It is a crazy time. Even people who pride themselves on their good judgment and composure can find themselves baring their very inebriated soul to a taxi driver and commiserating on the selfishness of men.

They can rediscover hangovers (not good) and Botox (actually surprisingly good) or dust off that old surfboard and rekindle their love for the water and solitude of going it alone. Maybe, like me, the vastness of options you discover after being cast out of the life you had known can be a frightening, powerful experience and one difficult to control.

Some people try to avoid the risk by refusing to deviate from their normal routine, attempting to stay rational, healthy, and stable, well away from the precipice of possibly losing control. However, by doing so, you may also miss an important phase of self-rediscovery. The shedding of the old and stepping into the new parts of yourself or those previously left behind can provide you with a new perspective. You may learn which of your parts you wish to keep and which do not fit anymore. By trial and error, you can gain new zest and vitality, self-direction, and confidence. Or possibly you are more like me: after being thrust out alone, I found some solace in sampling the vast array of pleasures I had thought were gone from my life forever. Solitude, self-indulgence, and fresh ideas for life are yours to take and the temptation to reach out is only heightened by the sense that you are "due" something for your pain and suffering. How do you find the best of what this time has to offer and reduce the risk that you will slip into recklessness?

Recognize Your Intentions

I believe the first step is to recognize and acknowledge your *intent*. If your intent is to hurt your partner, make them jealous, or threaten them with your independence, then you may not truly experience the benefits of this unique time in your life. Trying to incite a reaction in someone else is not the same as acting with intention and purpose. You would be basing your choices on someone else rather than on your own sense of rightness or desire. So my suggestion is to be authentic. Do whatever you sense is right and good and worthwhile and let that be the source of your power rather than trying to control someone else.

The second suggestion is to know yourself, your values, and your vulnerabilities and take steps to safeguard your physical, spiritual, social, and mental well-being. Before you begin this wild journey, take some time to think about what could hurt you, and minimize that risk. You want to be there for your kids, your family, and certainly yourself, so take some care. Create rules that you can commit to following and don't deviate. Only then you can let your intuition guide you without risking what is most important—your own health and safety.

Your rules should reflect what you hold as important and those things you do not wish to experience. For example, if you are a person of a particular faith and believe sex is only is to be enjoyed in marriage, then create a rule that stays true to that value. If you worry about your drinking, set limits or at least put the taxi service on your speed dial and vow to use it without fail. If you have children, create boundaries between "adult time" and "parent time"; be there for your kids and provide them the attention and care they need. The last thing you need right now is to feel bad or shameful for trying out new things and making mistakes, because there are sure to be a few. Just make them livable mistakes and ones that you can look back on with compassion and a healthy dose of humor.

Romance and Sex?

I should probably also introduce the elephant in the room: What about romance? Dating? Sex? Now many of you are loudly protesting, "Not for years! I can't even imagine being with someone else!" Okay, but let's talk about these issues anyway. One thing about being rejected is that it makes it very easy to want to be wanted. A partner's betrayal or indifference can create a vulnerability that, although easy to deny when alone, is difficult to ignore when unexpectedly meeting someone who expresses interest or desire for closeness.

It is not a bad idea to look inward and see if you are vulnerable. If so, acknowledge this as a very human state—we all want to be loved and feel closeness again. However, also recognize that your judgment is probably a bit challenged during this time. It's easy to try to recapture what you lost or let the pendulum completely swing in the opposite direction and search for what was missing in your last relationship. It is a common fantasy to think that the ending of your relationship is an opportunity to find the "right one" who will rescue you from all the pain and fear you are feeling right now. A new relationship may very well be in your future, but you will probably you have a lot to do before you are ready for a healthy one. And if you dive into something new too soon, you will deny yourself the opportunity to get to know the most important person: you.

Even just having sex without a relationship can be tricky. Maybe you were able to do so without any harm previously, but you are more vulnerable now than you have been in the past. Only you know if you would feel regret or exhilaration after being with someone new. Take a moment to be clear and respect your openness or new limitations. Think about good and not-so-good outcomes and create healthy boundaries for yourself or conditions that can protect you from risking your health or feeling anxiety, sadness, or shame. This time is all about giving yourself space, but you want to make sure that you fall off the curb, not the cliff. To find ways to ensure that your crazy time is filled with fun minus the fear, you might want to try the following exercise.

CHAPTER 6 EXERCISES: YOUR VALUES AND VULNERABILITIES

Take a moment to think about your personal values and your vulnerabilities. Think about what actions might cause you distress, embarrassment, or even shame. Those are the things to avoid if you are going to make this a time for safe exploration.

1. Make a list of the values, roles, or other things you most wish to protect (e.g., faith, finances, safety, sobriety).
2. When considering your vulnerabilities and strengths, what might challenge these important parts of your life?
3. Create a "no-go" list of simple rules or commitments that protect you from actions and choices that would be harmful to you. Protect yourself . . . but don't create an extremely limiting set of rules. Remember this is a time for stretching and give yourself room to enjoy some new experiences.
4. Know your guidelines well enough that you don't have to think in the moment and commit to following them faithfully. Oh, and have some fun! You deserve it.

CHAPTER 7

Sharing the News and Getting Support

THE TRANSITION FROM keeping silent about the painful state of your marriage to letting others know about the breakup can be difficult and awkward. It is hard to allow it to become real by speaking about it. It is also difficult to break the bonds of intimacy and let others in on what was once the most private of relationships. There may be a fear that you are, in fact, participating in the end of your relationship by sharing your struggles. Perhaps with each telling, the trauma is lived anew, and your attempts to answer the inevitable questions only deepen your own sense of sadness and confusion.

However, saying nothing and pretending all is well to coworkers, acquaintances, and extended family members has its own set of pitfalls. The question "What did you guys do this weekend?" becomes a landmine. You may determine to smile and drag your empty shell of a self through meetings and social engagements only to find yourself uncontrollably sobbing to your office mate. It is all so confusing, exposed, and, well, horribly messy. You may even think everyone is looking at you strangely.

Close friends and family can be a lifeline one moment and a liability the next. They may take your anger and sadness and raise the ante with their own rage or fear, leaving you to take care of your supposed comforters. Some mothers may worry about you without a man to care for you, which only heightens your own fears and undermines your sense of competency and confidence. Fathers may fly into a protective rage as if you were an adolescent and not a grown woman. Friends may say they never liked your husband in the first place, which doesn't really make you feel any better. Rather, it makes you feel even further from the life you once thought you had. You may experience none of these things, and if so, you are blessed. However, if you do, remember that friends and family are grieving and uncertain too.

Parents and Family

Even though you are at the center of this storm, your separation or divorce not only intimately affects your life but it also affects those closest to you. Parents and other family members may be shocked and grieved by losing someone they had welcomed into their lives. They may feel betrayed or filled with fear at the loss of security and relationship for you and, if you have kids, their grandchildren. They may worry about their own financial or emotional ability to support you if needed. In this way, their security is threatened, as well. They may be going through the same journey as you are: trying to make sense of the breakup and figuring out what went wrong. They may also focus on trying to fix what is broken to spare you heartache. You might need to relive the endless questions for which you have no answer. You may even find yourself in the odd position of calming their anger, instead of venting yours, or comforting their sadness even when it threatens to envelop you.

It may be hard for you to extend some patience and understanding, given your own state of distress, but family members may also need some time to get their bearings before developing skills that can effectively help you. Understand that they may not give the perfect comfort, initially, due to their own processing. You might need some time to clarify what is theirs to handle and keep it separate from your own stuff.

If you don't have children, the main issue is helping your family learn how to help you. You may need to tell them what you need directly or ask them to refrain from doing what is not helpful. I don't know if you have a mother like mine, but if anyone hurts Grandma June's kin, they will have a long, long road back to redemption. My mother's anger was understandable but not very helpful, because I spent much of my time managing her anger rather than expressing my own. I ended up comforting rather than being comforted, and I was consumed with worry that my parents might not only be unable to help me but also, given their age, would not be able to make it through this difficult time.

Your Besties

Much like your family, your closest friends may desperately want to help, yet they may little or no idea of what you need. Those with no experience with separation or divorce may lack the ability to understand the complexity of your emotions, such as failing to recognize that your anger may also be the outward expression of deep sadness and longing. Or they may simply feel more comfortable with some emotions but not others. One friend may connect only with the sadness, while another relentlessly attempts to find ways to "fix" what is wrong and repair the relationship rather than being present and meeting you however you are in the moment.

Friends' reactions are a combination of not only your situation but also their own needs, worries, comfort level, and awareness. Friends may feel confused by your fluctuating moods, feeling that you seem distant and isolated one moment but pleading for their company at the next. You may find that some moments you wish to talk endlessly about your pain and then suddenly feel an overwhelming wave of fatigue that settles over you like a heavy blanket. Then you just want to be alone or asleep or doing anything other than what you are doing. There may be times of weightlessness, of almost manic cheer, where you feel miles away from all of your suffering.

Friends may find it a relief that you, too, are unsure and you don't expect them to read your mind, be the perfect comforter, or fix your predicament. It may be important to explain that their willingness to listen is enough, that to be open to what you might need and to love you though the craziness of this time is deeply appreciated. These are your safe people you can utilize when testing out your new skills of focusing on your own needs and asking for help. If you are feeling isolated or exhausted and unable to reach out, you might want to ask them to call you once a week to check in or have a standing weekly date.

If you want to vent but don't want them to carry your anger or do anything that could endanger your future relationship with your partner, let them know. If you want to talk about anything but the suffering and feel part of the normal world for one evening, tell them so. If you need a partner in new adventures, ask them for their participation. If you want them to lay off the advice giving and just be present, be direct. It's that simple. If you don't ask, they won't know. And if you ask and they fall short, then at least you have a clearer idea of the support they can offer and what is beyond them to give. It may be incredibly important for you to know who you can rely on during this time. As hard as it may be to feel the disappointment, it is worse to not know who you can truly be yourself with and feel safe.

If you feel yourself hesitating or not wanting to "burden" others with your suffering, I would challenge you to consider what a friend in your position would welcome from you. If you're the type of person who is always helping, consider that helping others makes one feel wanted and needed; try allowing your friends the same opportunity. If you feel that you might overwhelm your friends, be open about it and reassure them that being honest about what they can and cannot give actually helps you find the courage to express what you need without hesitating in order to protect them from overextending themselves.

Mutual Friends

Friends who are mutual to both you and your partner can be tricky to navigate. You'll wonder how much to share and which "side" they might choose. You wonder what they know and understand about the state of your relationship and how it affects their perception of you and the future of your friendship with them. What were once pleasant, easy, fun-filled relationships could now be filled with anxiety.

Having some empathy for how your mutual friends feel can be useful in managing these situations. They may be struggling with how to keep connected to both of you, as well as how to be honest and broach the subject of your relationship without disrespecting either of you. Invitations to dinner or parties could become tension filled: Do they invite both of you and risk being disrespectful of your situation, or should they invite only one of you—and if so, which one? They may wonder how not to take sides or whether they can continue both relationships at all. Will they need to choose one friendship over the other? If it is a couple, they may have different relationships with each of you, which can cause tension in their own relationship. They could also be grappling with the anxiety that discussions surrounding your marriage arouse, such as the vulnerability of their own relationship to separation and divorce.

The very real fact is that people often take sides, and it may not be with the one they feel is "in the right" but is possibly based on social ties or the history and depth of friendship. Knowing and accepting that mutual friends are confused and anxious about the tangle of conflicting loyalties can make a world of difference. It helps keep you from taking their decisions too personally. Yes, it will hurt if some relationships change or end, but if you view their decision as a moral judgment rather than a difficult and nuanced personal decision, you are likely to feel it's a judgment about your value as a friend.

In my own experience, I have had people I once counted as friends change or end our relationships. I also found myself needing to do the same and let go of friendships or shift them to create a less intimate connection. My empathy for our friends came from my own realization that during the time of my divorce and becoming independent, I needed a greater sense of security and safety in those with whom I chose to spend time and share my thoughts. It was not in any way a judgment of their value to me, their goodness, or whose "team" they were on. It was simply an acknowledgement of my very honest need to feel safe in being myself and not feeling the presence of my ex in my closest relationships. It had to do with the anxieties that I could feel when I was with mutual friends.

Being sure of who was truly my friend without entanglements gave me the stability and safety I needed during the time of personal upheaval. This came hand in hand with knowing that I, at times, was unable to contain my feelings and words. I hold no ill will toward any of those people who are no longer close friends. I believe them to be good, caring, and fun people whom I do truly miss. Yet I understand that, like me, they had difficult choices to make and needed to move forward, just as I did. What I needed was to be my authentic self and share my feelings and experiences without censoring myself to protect others.

Looking back, I wish that I had done a better job of explaining those things to the people I moved away from. It is what I suggest to many of my clients in the same situation. Say the unspoken words, acknowledge the difficulty of their position, and let them know you will respect their decisions, even if it means changing the relationship with you or your ex. Being honest and allowing your friends to be honest in return can alleviate a lot of misinformation and needless misunderstandings. That way, no matter what happens, you can be sure that the friends you do keep are truly supportive and the ones you lose will hold respect and appreciation for your understanding.

You may feel great sadness, but you can also feel self-respect and dignity for handling a difficult situation with compassion and grace.

Focus on old and new relationships that meet your needs for authentic and enduring connections.

Acquaintances

I remember being surrounded by members of my son's co-op daycare shortly after I understood my marriage was ending. Couples and moms were setting playdates and forging new family friendships. I was terrified of being asked out to dinner with another couple or the inevitable questions about whether my husband and I were planning for more children. The disparity between the private sorrows in my home life juxtaposed with the joy of the growing families sitting around me at circle time was a struggle each and every day.

I felt the secret pain of knowing my child was facing a much different future than many other children would; hearing about family vacations that were no longer a part of my future made me sad. I am generally an open and honest person, yet my desire to be authentic was tempered by my fear of being judged. This brittle tension probably made me appear less than approachable and only added to my sense of isolation. My insecurity and lack of clarity about the "proper" course to take in disclosing my situation was not, I found, unique.

One client described a similar work issue to mine. Initially, she simply left out any reference to her husband, who had moved out the previous month, when discussing her social life. However, over time, the coworkers asked direct questions about what she and her husband had done over the weekend or their plans. Caught in the moment, she lied. She felt bad about lying, which only added to her sense of shame and isolation.

In our sessions, she struggled with whether or not she had the right to decide how much information to share. On the one hand, she hated being dishonest, but on the other, she wondered why she had to share this personal information. She feared it might have ramifications on her work and others' perception of her personally and professionally. She worried that her façade would crumble, but she also worried that if she disclosed her breakup, her coworkers would feel sorry for her or even question her ability to do her work.

To Share or Not to Share

The three very real questions to ask when deciding to tell people about the separation or divorce are:

1. Is the disclosure intended for your benefit or for others'?
2. What do *you* need? Will telling bring you closer or further from meeting that need?
3. Are there any possible negative consequences of sharing?

I believe the answers to these questions make the decision to share or not share pretty straightforward. Unless you have a deep relationship—which doesn't truly fit the whole acquaintance category—you do not need to share.

You have the right to separate your personal and professional life and move through your workdays with relative freedom from personal scrutiny. You may, in fact, need the distraction of work as a place where you can escape from the complexities and feel competent and productive. If that is what you need, then you have the right to keep things to yourself.

However, if you find your personal life spilling over into your work life and feel the need to explain in order to create some leeway in your duties, to get some time off, or simply to find support from those who could be helpful, then by all means feel free to share. The defining factor is that it is your choice, and it should be based on your needs, not on guilt for nondisclosure. Take care to decide objectively who is safe to tell or needs to know. You have a right to protect yourself, and just because you tell one person, it doesn't mean you need to tell everyone.

The same is true for social relationships. You retain the right to share or withhold your own personal experiences. You deserve the right to mingle among the "living" and leave your troubles for another time. However, if you find that, perhaps after a few drinks, you are suddenly sobbing or spilling your sad tale and begin to feel exposed, or if, looking back, you are embarrassed by your behavior, it might be helpful to have a brief statement of explanation that also provides some closure to the conversation. I mean one that leaves you feeling more centered and comfortable for future interactions.

It might be something to the effect of: "I'm going through a difficult time and although I am generally fine, sometimes the feelings just break through. I appreciate your understanding, but know that I'm okay." Even if you don't offer an explanation or if you never have the chance to see the person again, don't let yourself feel bad. You're human and you have the right to fall apart now and then in ways that aren't destructive to you or anyone else. And being embarrassed is not the worst thing in the world.

This is something I know well, and I can only thank the kindly older Norwegian gentleman at the bar who comforted me so sweetly (with the very few English words he knew) as I sobbed in the parking lot. I chose to accept his graciousness as a sign of the capacity for others to show compassion when needed, even if he thought I was just a wee bit crazy.

So what do you tell people when you decide it is good for you to share? First, you may want to take a moment and decide *why* you feel the need to disclose. Doing so makes it easier for you to double-check for the right intentions. It will also help determine what you wish to share. If your purpose is to offer an explanation to those who may be affected by changes in your mood, behavior, productivity, or need for special requests, then a simple explanation will do. You might want to explain the basic situation as, "I am having difficulties in my marriage, and there has been a separation." You might also explain what it is that you need/

don't need: "It's extremely stressful, but I am managing and taking care of myself. Still, I may need to take some vacation time or not take on any extra duties for a while."

You may also want to give them permission to address any problems or concerns with you directly rather than worry needlessly that you are not performing up to par. "I'll be open and ask directly for any support or allowances that I need, but if anything concerns you, I would really appreciate your direct feedback." That's about it in terms of making sure your bases are covered at work. Still, it is up to you if you wish to share more. More than likely, people you aren't close to probably don't want to hear all of the details, and if they do, it might not be for the right reasons. If you feel that people are asking for details you would rather not share, it's a good idea to have a response ready that respectfully conveys your personal boundaries, such as, "I'm touched by your concern, but I really enjoy coming to work (or going out, if it's social) and putting all the negative stuff aside."

The safest bet is to tell people less about what is happening and more about what you need from them or what you need in the situation. People will most likely be glad to have your direction in setting the tone for a difficult subject, which alleviates their anxiety about how to interact with and support you.

I also want to mention that after disclosing the basics, there is sometimes the tendency to follow up with more information than you intended to share. There is a lot of stigma to the big "D," and it is understandable not to wish to be associated with those negative stereotypes. However, in attempting to protect yourself from other people's judgment, you may find yourself moving way past your comfort zone, where you begin to feel exposed and vulnerable.

In attempting to convey your values or lack of power to save your marriage, you also open the door to portraying yourself as "the victim" or "the lady with the sad story." This may unintentionally make you feel you are the subject of sympathy or even pity, which comes with its own stigma. So be honest with yourself about why you are disclosing and ask yourself if those who are not intimately associated with you need to know the details of your personal life. Perhaps it can deepen relationships, but maybe you need to look to your closer, safer relationships or a professional to validate your feelings and meet your need for understanding and guidance.

What to Expect

When Sara broke the news of her impending divorce to her bewildered father, she experienced a similar situation of having to manage his reaction. Her father vowed to "crush" her husband in the legal arena and make him pay for what he had done. Although the show of protection was well intentioned, and Sara certainly wasn't feeling any sympathy for her soon-to-be ex, as a parent she knew that a hostile relationship with her children's father was not in their best interest. Sara acted quickly to tell her father that seeking retribution was not supporting her and that, ultimately, she wanted to have a civil relationship with the father of her children. She told him that instead she longed for a safe place to escape from time to time and asked for some financial help so she and her children could take some much-needed trips home to visit. He was more than willing, and he appreciated a specific request that allowed him to feel he was acting positively for his daughter in her time of need.

If you have children, the relationships they have with other family members are extremely important for their ability to cope well in the future. The prospect of divorced parents is painful enough. Their lives will change in ways that they did not want or expect. Yes, if you divorce, your children will have two separate homes and separate relationships with each parent. Those are changes that may be a part of their future, but if access to one or both parents is threatened or relationships with other loving family members are severed, that is severely damaging to children.

Even though your partner is leaving you, it does not mean they are leaving your children. Yes, what they are doing is hurtful, but unless they actually abandon the children or refuse to take part in their care, they probably have every intention and desire to continue parenting. I say that directly because it is important to recognize the boundary between your marriage relationship and the parenting relationship. In your pain, you may struggle to make sense of that, and your family members may too. You might not feel like it now, but making this co-parenting commitment will be one of the most important things you can do for your children's long-term well-being: don't undermine—or let family members undermine—any parental relationship, limit parent access, or contaminate special events with conflict.

Your friends and family will look to you to set the standard of what is acceptable and not acceptable. If you can manage to behave respectfully toward your children's father when it counts, then your parents and family members should be able to muster the strength on the infrequent occasions when they are called to do so. I clearly remember my anxiety preparing for my son's second birthday party, which was the first since the separation. This may not be a choice many people make, but we had always celebrated with family and I wanted to continue the tradition. The phone call with my mother was pretty direct. I let her know it was okay if she was mad and hurt, but it was not okay to let her feelings undermine her grandchild's enjoyment of his special day.

I told her I wanted her there, but only if she was confident that she could be respectful. I told her that I would politely ask *her*, not my son's father, to leave if it became apparent she could not do so. I also expressed the same sentiment to my friends. I am grateful my mother graciously understood my request and behaved wonderfully at the party. She now heartily embraces the peaceful culture of inclusion we enjoy at all our family gatherings and has expressed her gratitude that I acted quickly to protect her grandchild's ability to enjoy his family during that difficult time.

Maybe sharing special events is not something that you expect or want for your family's future. Still, whatever you choose, it is important to take the initiative and be clear with friends and family as to your expectations for their behavior and sharing of information that could be potentially hurtful to your children or their other parent. You may wish to explain that your intention is to protect your children and their relationships with the people they love and offer ideas of how you would like them to interact at family events or when children are likely to overhear or otherwise become privy to information.

You can also explain when it is safe to "talk adult," but you may wish to ask that those conversations are kept private. For example, it might be just fine to vent and rant about your ex when it's just you and Mom or with friends on a night out, but it stays between you; the rules are different when it potentially involves kids or the other parent. Creating some common sense boundaries with those close to you can not only help them know how to best support you but also how to join you in protecting your children's childhood and preserving their loving relationships.

Can They Handle It?

Some family members are unable to handle the information without their reactions causing more distress. Claire's grandmother was elderly and in ill health. Claire decided not to tell her grandmother about her separation because it would likely cause her so much distress that her health could be in jeopardy. Besides, Claire realized that she could enjoy and take solace in her grandmother's company even if her grandmother was unable to offer support for the separation. She was also quite confident her grandmother would not accidentally learn about it, given that she generally visited her grandmother without her husband anyway.

If you find that you are routinely comforting another or managing that person's reactions rather than receiving support, it may be that they simply do not have the capacity to hear or respond in ways that meet your needs or prevent escalating conflict. Have you tried giving them specific direction, and it hasn't helped? It's not necessary to judge—everyone has his or her limit or issues they just can't navigate in healthy ways.

If this is the case, it may be helpful to clearly acknowledge that fact and decide what you feel would be the best solution. It could be that you limit certain types of information or generally cut down on the frequency or amount of information disclosed—it's up to you. Just as with acquaintances and friends, you aren't responsible for sharing equally or everything just because these people are family. It is more important to take steps to care for yourself and your children than to meet someone else's desire to be kept up to date with all the details. They may not understand why you're holding back, but that is just one more indication that they could lack insight into how their actions or words negatively affect you. Some people might actually have some insight into their own triggers and can be receptive to you honestly telling them your concerns and your plan to back off certain information. For instance, you might tell your sister, the financial analyst, that every time you share information about the financial settlement, she goes into analyst mode when you really just crave sister-to-sister talk. People can understand better when you can acknowledge their good intentions and reassure them that there are other ways you value their comfort.

You are the best one to make that call and you may have to decide, based on your knowledge of the person and the depth of relationship, whether it is worth having that conversation. Perhaps simply using what is in your power to solve the situation is preferable. Your situation is bound to be unique. It is a good idea to complete the following exercises to clarify what you want most from your family and what power you have to protect that future vision.

CHAPTER 7 EXERCISES: GROUND RULES FOR FRIENDS AND FAMILY

Take some time to write about what is most important to you and/or your family, as well as the specific things you want when you are on the other side of this journey. Focus on several areas:

1. Write a statement about what you want for yourself as an individual, such as respect, peaceful parenting without conflict, financial security, or to be happy again, etc.
2. Write a statement about what you want for your children, such as good relationships with both parents and the extended family, feeling financially and emotionally supported, not feeling separate in two different homes, etc.
3. If you feel ready, write what you want for your soon-to-be ex, such as growing as a parent, feeling comfortable at special events, feeling comfortable sharing and receiving parenting information, etc.
4. Identify those things that will help and the things that might challenge meeting your goals.
5. Looking back on your statements of intention and the list of challenges, create a few basic but specific rules or boundaries to help ensure success and minimize challenges.
6. Identify the people with whom you will likely need to address these issues. Decide whether you are going to offer direct guidance in the form of boundaries or whether you need to act independently by limiting information or access in order to safeguard your well-being or family relationships. Write your intentions for action that each individual may need to take.

CHAPTER 8

The Ghost in the House: Living with Your Soon-to-Be Ex

THE SPACE BETWEEN knowing a divorce is imminent and before one of you leaves the home is what one client so perfectly referred to as "living with the ghost in the house." He looks like your partner, sometimes even acts like your partner, yet if you were to try to reach out to him, you'd feel that there is nothing solid to grasp, only empty air. It may be brutally uncomfortable, with silence and arguments. Your feelings of grief may surface unexpectedly, triggered by necessary interactions with your partner as you go about the business of living side by side yet so far apart. But surprisingly, some people actually get along better, with less tension at times, which marks the beginning of detachment from the old rules, old patterns, and arguments.

Even though you still need to manage the same tasks as before, it becomes abundantly clear that the old ways of doing things can lead to emotional landmines. The need to parent, pay the bills, make the meals, and manage the home all coexist with the need to grieve. How do you find comfort and solace when the person who did the hurting brushes past you in the kitchen? How do you fulfill everyday responsibilities that were once done with a generous heart when the shared goal of family is gone? How do you let go of some of those duties, especially when it comes to your children, when there is no more trust and yet your partner wants to "become more involved"? How do you keep things the same for your children when everything else is changing?

The answers are difficult: they involve learning what you need, renegotiating old arrangements, and creating space for yourself that is independent of your partner and allowing your partner to do so as well. As counterintuitive as it may seem, just when you want connection and everything to stay the same, you may need to step back from the relationship to find some space for standing on your own. You need boundaries, a new and clear set of expectations that can guide you during one of the most confusing times in divorce.

There are no black-and-white rules for navigating this painful time, but it is well worth the effort to ask yourself and your partner what is and is not acceptable: What will keep hurt and conflict to a minimum and begin building more respectful interactions during the time you are still living together? It's not about revenge or trying to poke each other's soft spots while you still have them in your sights. It's about what it is you truly need in order to feel okay and then asking your partner to respect your needs.

Grief and Comfort

After six months of marriage counseling, Nancy's husband told her he was done and wanted a divorce. That was two months ago. Unable to figure out the next step to take, they were continuing to live in the same home with their two children. Nancy was frequently crying herself to sleep before Rob came to bed.

In our session, Nancy began to sob, "It's like he doesn't even care about me as a human being anymore. He sees me crying, and he can't even hug me or hold me." From Rob's perspective, he hated that he was causing his wife so much pain. He did, in fact, think of holding her but pushed the inclination away, believing that it would be unwanted and would provoke her anger even more. He also worried that if she did accept his comfort, she might take his gesture of concern as something deeper than sympathy and did not want to give her false hope.

When we explored this issue, Nancy did admit that she likely would have taken his hug as an invitation for the intimacy that she so desperately wanted. She came to a better understanding of how something so natural and simple between them had now become so complicated with the change in their relationship. By honestly acknowledging the change, Nancy could create boundaries that protected her when she was most vulnerable. She acknowledged that doing so "felt like giving up in a way, like I am accepting what's happening when everything in me wants to fight it." Still, it was her first step in standing her ground and honoring her need to grieve and get support in ways that would truly be sustaining rather than hurtful.

Daily Tasks and Responsibilities

As Nancy began to care for herself and not solely for the relationship, she noticed other areas that needed to change, and she continued to acknowledge them openly and directly from a place of independence and strength. One area was daily routines she had been doing for years without any issue. One night when Rob called to say he would be working and would not be home till late, she was in the middle of preparing dinner, cleaning the house, and getting the kids' homework going after her own busy workday. Nancy realized that although this had been commonplace during their marriage (Rob made more money, and she had more time, so it had all worked out—until now), she now needed some time away from the kids.

She just needed a break and was resentful that he continued to assume she would take sole responsibility for childcare. Nancy spoke up and asked Rob to make a temporary schedule for who was "on duty" and who was "off duty" to care for the kids. It was a novel concept for Rob, and it took some reminders and Nancy standing her ground, but in the end, Rob realized it was one of the changes that needed to happen if he were to take a greater role in his children's daily needs.

Even without children, is it fair that the old routines continue, such as who does the laundry, the cleaning, or the bills? What about abrupt changes in the rules? Is it okay if, now that the "divorce" word has been spoken, one of you stays out all night while you are still living in the family home? It's complicated, and all of these issues will need to be addressed while you still living together.

If you like making the dinner, then perhaps you are fine with continuing to do so. If you want to give or get hugs, cry in each other's arms—that is your call, as long as you are mindful of the effect it has on not only you but also your partner. You may decide on one set of rules and then make changes based on new information as you learn it. The following are some areas that commonly lead to disagreements and misunderstandings and some prompting questions that can help you determine your boundaries.

CHAPTER 8 EXERCISES: CREATING HEALTHY BOUNDARIES

You and your partner may have very different needs or views, but answering the following questions gives you a starting point for considering solutions to difficult interactions or tasks as you begin to clarify your boundaries. It may be helpful to do the exercise in sections slowly over time, or simply use it to understand what you need right now. However, if you intend to share these with your partner, it may be helpful to get support in creating a safe and productive setting to have these discussions.

Relationship Issues

1. When is it okay to talk about your relationship, and when is it not okay?
2. How do you want to handle friends? Is it okay to go out with mutual friends without the other's knowledge? Are any friends of particular concern?

3. What information do you share with friends or family members who interact with the two of you or your children? Any information to be kept private?
4. How much personal interaction are you comfortable with? What about touching?

Daily Life and Finances

1. Which daily tasks do you feel comfortable keeping? Any that you feel need to be altered or shared? How and why?
2. What kind of information sharing is needed? Should you share where you will be? Be available to contact? What are your expectations for privacy?
3. What are your financial expectations? Should there be an understanding regarding spending large sums of money? How much?
4. When things get heated or overwhelming, how could you let the other person know without escalating conflict? How can you respectfully take a time-out, and how long can you be gone?

Parenting

1. How will you both continue to meet your children's daily needs? Will you take turns?
2. If you plan to share parenting duties, what will your schedules be? What will you do if there are conflicts with scheduling (e.g., how you will ask and whether the other parent can decline)?
3. Where will the off-duty parent go? Do they have access to the home?
4. What are the on-duty parent's and off-duty parent's expectations for contact and/or privacy?

PART TWO

Putting It Back Together: Redefining Yourself and Your Family

CHAPTER 9

Separation: When Change Becomes Real

THIS IS A POINT in time where the changes often become very real. Unless there is talk of reconciliation, one partner often begins to take steps to leave the home—or both partners begin to grapple with how to untangle living together as a family. Up until this point, even if changes have been discussed and fought over, as painful as they were, they remained ideas pinned in the future rather than concrete realities.

Separation affects parents differently than it does for people without children. For parents, a physical separation marks the beginning of a different relationship: changing from the adult relationship of spouses to the child-centered relationship of co-parents. Given the different challenges and tasks, let's consider each one individually.

Challenges for Separated Partners Without Children

For those without children, separation may be a jarring, hard stop of a transition. For better or worse, up until now your partner was likely present, and you had the opportunity to speak to them and experience their reactions. When one of you leaves, the empty space can be filled with silence or one-sided discussions with yourself. You may miss the connection to your partner, even if it was pain, anger, or sadness that connected you. The contact you do have may vary.

For some, the legal process or negotiating the practicalities is the only chance to connect, and it can feel like a cold, business-like way to experience the end of the relationship. For others, it can be a flash point and become a way for either or both of you to express what remains of the relationship through decisions or items that symbolize pain and anger.

Some others may have the opportunity to speak on a regular basis as they process the end of relationship, and it is up to you to decide if contact is helpful or hurtful. Having contact with your ex may be something you find helpful in your process of grief. It may offer you a way to keep the good parts of the relationship and tether your past to the future. It may offer you insight into what happened and allow you to integrate that information into your life story as you move forward.

However, you also might find that it is not helpful. Grief, anger, or sadness can be triggered by the contact and prevent you from moving forward. Only you can decide. My advice is that if contact is an option, be sensitive of how you feel before, during, and after contact. Is the relationship transforming into something new—based on respect, honor, and kindness—or does it remain static and unchanged from the way it was during your marriage? Do you feel on equal footing or pulled back into experiencing the pain of being the one who was left?

The former is much more indicative of a healthy and sustaining reason for continued contact than the latter. If contact isn't an option, remind yourself that it is more likely due to their needs or emotional experience than anything about you. Those who choose to end a relationship often find it difficult to face the consequences of that choice in the other person—or even perhaps within themselves. Accept that you may never truly know what was in their heart and mind, focus on being compassionate about what you've had to endure, and create the life you deserve in the future.

Challenges for Separated Parents

A separation stage marks the beginning of building the foundation for planning the long-term parenting of their children through their childhood and significant life events. Not only will parents need to discuss difficult decisions about the separation and divorce, they will also have to continue to communicate on some level for the rest of their children's lives to support them across two households.

Parents who have held off talking to their children must now prepare them for the upcoming changes in their lives. They need to explain one parent's absence from the home and reassure their children about how their family will function and when they will spend time with each parent. Each person will have to grapple with the reality of being apart from their children when they are with the other parent.

Some parents might have the ability to manage communication about the kids in a clear and businesslike way, but many do not, and the strain and anxiety regarding the future, plus the fears for how children will navigate the changes, can make even the most level-headed parent wary and frightened.

Some parents enter this stage weary and emotionally raw and may react to any changes with a fierce need to protect. It can often result in one or both parents reacting by digging in their heels and finding their positions in the fight to protect their parenting and their children.

In the following chapters, I offer a much deeper look at how having children affects the experience of separation and divorce. Although my role as a therapist is often to help children through a divorce, my goal here is not to cover exhaustively how children are affected, what they need, and how to create parenting agreements. There are books that can offer you that information; some of my favorites are listed in the Resources section of the book.

Rather, for those with children, my goal is to provide you with some basic child-centered information to help you navigate through your own emotional process in ways that can support your attempts to problem solve with the other parent and support your children. I want to help point to the reasons why it is so common for child issues to cause so much anxiety and conflict during this period, and help you to distinguish where you might be right to be concerned and when it is okay to relax and accept the changes that may be normal and expected.

CHAPTER 9 EXERCISES: ONGOING COMMUNICATION DECISIONS

This exercise is meant to help clarify your wishes about maintaining ongoing communication–and, if so, for how long and what purpose. If you don't have children, the choice is really up to you, but parents will need to have ongoing communication with each other about their children. Use this exercise to help you decide whether ongoing communication is helpful or [if it's necessary] how to communicate in ways that maximize productivity and minimize conflict or hurt. Take a few deep breaths and consider the following questions:

1. As you think back on the last few interactions you've had with your ex, write down the first few emotions/thoughts that come to mind.
2. List your goals for these interactions, such as decision making, getting information, expressing feelings, validation of feelings, etc.
3. Were your goals met? Did you get what you needed?
4. What insight does this exercise provide about your communications? Are they helpful/hurtful or productive/unproductive? Are there types of communication or topics that are better or worse? Why?
5. List any practical, defined reasons to communicate.
6. Describe any consequences of ceasing communication. If you have children, consider this question carefully and include how they could be affected by limiting or ceasing communication.

7. Given your answers, do you intend to continue communication? If it is your intent to cease communication, skip to #10. If you intend to have ongoing communication, continue on to #8.
8. Looking at the reasons in favor of ongoing communication, consider the different methods: email, text, phone, and in person. The different methods are listed in order of how each lies along the continuums of "businesslike/personal" and "predictable/unpredictable." The choice of methods gives you options that fit either your need for emotional safety or tolerance for contact while meeting your goals for communication. Considering this, on a horizontal sheet of paper, make three columns. List your goals for communication on the left. In the middle column, note the mode you could use. Use the space in the right column to note how effective that method may or may not be.
9. If you decide to cease contact, list your reasons on another page (such as how it helps and what it avoids) as a reminder of your intentions.
10. Keep your list handy to track how you feel before, during, and after any communication. The list can also help you determine whether your goals are being met over time or be used as a reminder of your goals for not communicating. As time goes on, continue to evaluate your communication strategies and make alterations or reconsider approaches, as needed.

CHAPTER 10

Co-Parenting Decisions and Conflict

IF YOU HAVE CHILDREN, the following questions are at the forefront of your mind day and night and can hit you in your most vulnerable places:

- ◊ How can you manage your children's grief when you struggle to manage your own?
- ◊ How can you protect them from something you cannot control?
- ◊ What pieces of their past should you fight to retain, and what do you have to accept as the inevitable changes divorce brings?

The Best Interests of the Children

During separation and divorce, parents can struggle with truly understanding the oft-used phrase, "What is in the best interests of my children?" My work as a child specialist in collaborative divorce proceedings and my own experience as a divorced parent have given me insight into the complexities and contradictions embodied in this particular phrase. Despite my years as a child therapist, I've experienced the anguish of knowing my child would face changes that would alter and complicate the course of his life. I feared he would not be the healthy, joyful, blissfully confident child I'd envisioned or seen when I was happily (or so I thought) married.

Many of my clients reflect the same fears and desperation, and often, just like me, they base their ideas about how to protect their children on emotions like fear, anger, and grief. Great parents with the best of intentions and with a fierce desire to do what is right for their kids can find themselves in high conflict under the guise of "fighting for their children" or "protecting their children," even if it means protection from their other parent.

Yes, there are things worth "fighting" for, such as significant safety concerns and your children's access to both parents' care and love, but I see people arguing that only *their* position is in the best interests of the child. I call this view a strategic or reactive mind-set. So if the other parent disagrees, he or she must not be "putting the kids first," and off they go. I was one of those parents for a while. Trying to argue about what is best for a child with a child therapist, I admit, was not a fair fight, and I (mostly unintentionally) used my expertise because I, like many parents, thought I knew best. I still believe I had many sound opinions, but I erred in believing that if my child's father did not agree with me, it meant he did not care about what was right for our son.

I refused to listen, and even when I did, I interpreted his motives as hurtful rather than as a valid perspective. I was fighting *for* my son by fighting *against* his own father, which was generally counterproductive and resulted in an impasse. I finally changed due to the insight I gained after these interactions: although I'd felt "right," I also felt a definite sense of guilt, and, for me, guilt means I need to pay attention. By exploring that guilt, I realized that my actions were in contrast to the person I had believed myself to be—fair, kind, and aware. I slowly realized that even though what had happened was unfair, it did not excuse my actions, and I ultimately could not rationalize the hard-line stances I had been taking.

I knew better and accepted I had a choice to make: stay true to the kind of person I thought I was and wanted to remain or continue to live in the bitterness. For many reasons, one of which was I just got tired of being angry, I salvaged my hope and pride and decided to move forward. Even though the hurt and anger didn't disappear, I no longer used it as my guide for relating with my ex or making decisions about our son.

In the end, we still disagree on some things. But I learned to listen and believe that he truly does love our son and want the best for him, despite the fact that we disagree on some core issues. When I shifted into this belief, it helped us to have productive discussions of substance rather than unproductive, hurtful arguments that did not serve our beautiful son.

In many cases, fighting over the best interests of the child can be a lot like the ironic saying: "Fighting for peace is like . . ." It really doesn't make much sense, since one of the biggest factors in how well children cope and adjust to divorce is the amount of conflict they are exposed to both during and after divorce. Although important, it's not perfect schedules that make the difference. It's not the bedtime rituals or the partner in the wings. It's how well their parents can minimize the conflict so the children's daily lives and loving relationships with both parents can continue without disruption.

Then what really is in the best interests of the children? I would love to answer that question. Many of the ideas that I have gathered in my work with children are woven throughout this book, as well as in *The Co-Parenting Handbook*. The ability to take care of yourself emotionally, do your own healing, and find ways to stay present and positive are, I believe, what makes it possible to respond to your children and meet their needs.

Reactive Mind-sets

One issue I witness with compassion in my practice is that parents can often become stuck in several reactive (strategic) mind-sets rather than developing an open mind and heart, which is essential to respectful cooperation and responding to their children with sensitivity and accurate empathy. Strategy is positional: the justification or explanation for why *your* opinion is the correct one and how you intend to go about persuading the other of your "rightness." That stance leaves little room for considering the other's perspective or listening to new ideas. This is not to say you can't have your opinions, but don't get locked in a position of aggressively pursuing your own agenda to the point where you lose the big picture of what you ultimately want in the long term.

One of the reasons people become stuck in reactive mind-sets, which they have to untangle later—or never untangle and forever subject their children to—is that they tend to remain stuck in their own explanations of the past. It's easier to project those explanations onto the future without allowing new information in, envisioning different ways of interacting, or taking new steps to change old patterns. How the partner behaved in the marriage or at the beginning of the divorce process becomes a reliable indicator of how they will feel, act, and think through the whole of the journey. Open yourself to the fact that it may not true in every case.

We take our emotions of hurt, anger, betrayal, and distrust from that intimate adult relationship and project it onto how we think the ex-partner will parent in the future. Interpreting the feelings and motivations of your partner too rashly and thinking of them as set in stone can give rise to the "good guy/bad guy," "victim/perpetrator," "good parent/bad parent" view.

Reactive Mind-set #1: Using Parenting Plans as Power

A parenting plan is an agreement between parents about how they are responsibly going to care for their children as they grow; sometimes this plan is part of a separation or divorce agreement. If feeling hurt and betrayed, it can be easy to channel those emotions into the decision-making process. Some parents can make the mistake of using residential and visitation schedules as a way to "punish" the other parent for leaving. Many times, the parent is unaware that they are utilizing this strategy.

It's more likely that fear and unresolved emotions led them to a strongly held conviction of the "right" solution. They can find ample evidence to support their position, whether from their experience with the ex-spouse or by well-intentioned culling of information about the children's needs and development. Usually it's more of a reverse-engineering approach rather than due to any malicious intent. Still, the results can fuel the fire of conflict and animosity and severely limit the ability to work with the other parent in ways that actually do help the children.

Traditionally, and still in many families, women and men divide their roles in a family down gender lines. The husband may be the one who provides financially, and the wife provides much of the childcare. This might work well in family life, but when it comes to divorce, gender may be the "corner" each partner moves to in a "fight."

This described Jeff and Monica's situation and, in a large part, resulted in conflict that threatened their family when creating a post-divorce life. Monica was a stay-at-home mom with three boys, while Jeff's role was working full-time at a large tech company. Things ran smoothly for thirteen years, and the family enjoyed the stability of a good income. The boys flourished with an attentive parent at home to meet their needs.

In divorce, however, the threat of shifting roles caused the greatest fear for Monica: she could not envision "giving up" her stay-at-home role and entering the workforce after neglecting her career for so many of her most productive years. Monica resisted any attempts to get her to step back from her "turf" and saw Jeff's attempts to parent as "losing ground." Her resistance, in turn, provoked Jeff's fear that he would lose his children due to his inability to be involved in their lives in any way other than as a visiting parent every other weekend.

Jeff's response was to move back to his position of power—money—and resist sharing the family's financial resources in any way that allowed Monica to continue being the primary parent. For this couple, the results were predictable. They fell into their strategy of holding on to what they felt they had most control over, and the parenting plan became a battleground for what was really an emotional argument based on fear. Monica feared the unknown of career, giving up her central role as a mom, and the challenges for her children's adjustment. Jeff feared being held infinitely responsible for all financial support and losing daily contact and a meaningful relationship with his children. Both parents were unable to step back from the precipice and hear the other's fears. They couldn't find ways to reassure each other while respectfully asserting their own needs.

Commonly, when parents are in conflict, their ultimate parenting agreement does reflect an acceptable balance, but that can come after much animosity that seriously batters important relationships. They find it after a financial cost that could have been used toward supporting the family's long-term goals. It isn't always possible to avoid conflict, but knowing the common fears and struggles of other parents may help you to challenge yourself and do your part to manage emotional struggles outside of the parenting plan negotiations. Focus on what you truly need to feel safe and spare your children the disruption of unnecessary prolonged legal battles.

Reactive Mind-set #2: His Decision, He Should Suffer

Being left can lead to a desire for justice, and some parents may take that stance when considering the parenting plan. It might feel good to be able to "call the shots" after being blindsided and betrayed. However hard it is, though, give some thought to the balance of not just the responsibility of the other parent but also his or her parental rights. It may seem too much to ask you to think about your ex's position; do they really deserve your consideration?

But if you want to ensure that the outcome of your agreement will last or that it offers your kids adequate access to the love and care of both of their parents, then yes, you must listen. You should also acknowledge (even if you don't agree with) the needs of your former partner. It may even surprise you that, at times, the decisions are not always win/lose. With some flexibility, win/win solutions can be found. In short, guilt and fear are not a good foundation for lasting agreements.

Janet thought that after the chaos of divorce, everything was finally going according to plan. Devastated when her husband unexpectedly left her, she found her footing after moving to a new community. Her ex-husband and father of her two children gave her pretty much anything she had asked for in the settlement. Although she did not intentionally strategize to use his guilt in her negotiations, she knew that it had a large part in his willingness to acquiesce to her proposals.

Since the separation, her two boys, ages eight and twelve, had expressed anger at their dad for "leaving them" and resisted the monthly weekend visits with him. By allowing them to reject visits with their father whenever they chose, she felt that she was only respecting their wishes and giving them some sort of control over their own lives after all the other changes. Lately, however, their father had been pressing for more time to reunite with the kids. He felt that their original agreement was unfair and bad for the boys' long-term well-being. Having the time to process his feelings post-divorce, he found he regretted the agreement he made when still consumed by guilt. Janet and her children's newfound stability seemed threatened just when she'd begun to relax, and she was torn between maintaining the consistency for her kids and once again having to negotiate with her ex.

Janet came to the office with a list of complaints against the children seeing their father—mostly along the lines of resisting additional change when, in her view, the boys were adjusting "just fine." Janet needed help to see that while *she* may have felt a sense of stability and well-being with little to no contact with her ex, her children would likely have significant long-term consequences by losing contact with their father. Initially resistant, Janet was eventually able to consider the effect on the boys and explore her anxieties that had little to do with the kids and much more to do with her own adult process of grief and fears around setting appropriate boundaries with her children. It also helped that Dad was able to resist his desire to "settle the score" and instead understood his ex-wife needed reassurances to calm her anxieties and become cooperative in supporting the boys in resuming their monthly visits, expanding their residential time, and repairing their relationship with Dad.

Reactive Mind-set #3: Bad Dad = Less Time and Involvement

This mind-set comes in many different flavors, which I will address separately. However, it is generally the view that fathers are not as caring, committed, and skilled or safe as mothers, and, therefore, the children need to be protected from too much of his time and involvement. The protective parent may be legitimately concerned that sharing parenting duties and time might result in emotional or physical neglect, disruptions in routines and decision making, or substandard day-to-day parenting.

Again, I am not trying to dismiss or minimize a parent's concern. But it is very difficult to distinguish between the overwhelming fear of the unknown or sadness over the change in the marriage relationship and well-founded, significant safety concerns in a parental relationship. Many people often become mired in the "stew" of their marriage and develop certain ways of being that must change when the relationship ends. Yes, that same support system is gone, but there is also freedom from old patterns and the opportunity to remake or improve what needed improvement as a parent. Sometimes, when we step out of the way, others have the room to step up. You never know.

The following are some of the "bad dad" views that commonly come up and can be difficult to navigate, and they could benefit from a little more positive or hopeful perspective.

"He never cared about spending time with the kids before, but now . . ."

In many marriages, parents have spoken or unspoken arrangements that guide their family life. For many, instead of each doing half of everything—the chores, the childcare, the finances, and everything else it takes to run a home—they each take on different full tasks. This often means that one parent contributes the majority of the financial support while the other maintains the flexibility and availability that is a part of meeting the children's varying needs.

Again, this is not true of all families, but it can be the key to a smooth, functioning family when done with a glad heart and with a feeling of partnership. When divorces happen, though, the roles people have worked hard to master and feel competent and satisfied doing can be threatened. The primary caretaker is suddenly terrified of being asked to give up or drastically change the role they believe in so strongly and have invested so much time and effort into for many years.

I know this may seem gender biased, but I'm going to say it anyway, even though there are many exceptions: in my experience, women are often these primary caretakers and rely on their husband as the primary financial support. In such cases, I often find these fathers attempting to become more involved or expressing their desire to become more involved with their children after the separation.

Although it seems like this would be a wonderful thing, it is often met with extreme resistance during divorce. "What does he think he's going to do?" questioned one mother, who'd only recently gone back to working part-time now that her children were all in school. "In the last ten years he barely spent any time with them, and *now* he wants to be a dad? He's clueless, and I'm not convinced he's doing this because he really *wants* the kids. This is more about hurting me by taking away what I have lived for these past ten years. I think it's probably because he doesn't want to look like a jerk or that he thinks it will mean he will owe less child support."

It can be very difficult to have much confidence that a parent who has not demonstrated a great deal of enjoyment and participation—in not just the fun times, but the everyday difficult ones—really knows how and genuinely wants to step into the real work and responsibility of parenting. Yes, it may be true that they don't know the first thing about the delicate dance of making lunches, arranging play dates, getting the kids to bed on time, remembering their friends, scheduling activities, or just remembering to bring that extra coat or snack. Your concern is perfectly understandable, given their inexperience.

The kids might feel awkward, and the other parent may struggle and fail to meet all your children's needs. However, many parents who have been less involved do realize that if they do not step up, they will lose their children in many ways or end up being excluded from important parts of their lives. A divorce forces them to see that the other person doesn't parent for them by proxy, and they may become motivated to take on those responsibilities.

One couple's exchange put into words the essential struggle. After a long diatribe about how the father had neglected the family for years, the mother pleaded, "Can't you just let me do what I do really well? Why do you want to take the kids away from me?"

The father replied, "You don't think the kids need me and that they are better off without me, which scares the hell out of me. If I leave it to you, I will lose my kids. They will not know me, and I won't be a father but a stranger. I know part of you is angry I couldn't do it when we were together, and I guess I deserve that, but now I feel I have to fight you to be allowed just to be a father."

His anguish was, in part, why he was stuck in wanting a 50/50 parenting schedule, despite his demanding work schedule. For him, it meant that he was just as important to his children as their mother was. Hearing and respecting the deep underlying reasons for his insistence of equal time with the children, even when she didn't agree, was the key to connecting with compassion and creating productive negotiations for them both. With his motive heard and understood, Mom was able to give concrete reassurance that she did respect his desire to parent and maintain his relationship with the kids with "enough" time and in meaningful ways. Dad was ultimately able to relax and move away from percentages so both could then focus on bringing their own resources to support the children rather than counting hours.

"If he cared about the kids, he wouldn't ask for any more changes."

Consistency is the key word for many parents who didn't initiate their separation or divorce. They don't want change. Hell, they didn't want the relationship to end. Isn't it okay to ask the other parent to make the least amount of change for everyone else involved? It sounds pretty reasonable, and it was one of the places where I became stuck, as well. Here I was, steeped in attachment parenting, making my own baby food and buying organic sheets, when suddenly I was faced with becoming a single parent. They didn't cover this in Lamaze.

What I didn't know then (but do now) is that children can deal with change as long as we help them and attend to their needs in a present, emotionally sensitive, and responsive manner. Change is inevitable in divorce. Most families do not have the resources to maintain many of the same routines and residential arrangements. Even when there are resources, changes may be desired by one or both parents or necessary to accommodate a two-home arrangement and allow children to maintain their relationship with both parents.

Maureen and Joseph were having problems with their temporary parenting plan. She felt that recent overnight stays at their father's new apartment were significantly distressing for the children. Joseph also acknowledged the kids having difficulties, but did not wish to give up his time with them. Maureen explained that the children wanted to refuse visits: "They beg me not to go. They love him, but I think they need to be at home more and go over for the evening, not overnight." There seemed to be no substantive reason for the children not liking it at Dad's, just that it seemed weird and they missed Mom.

What came out was that Maureen herself was having a hard time with the changes. Her kids were, too—they, like most children, did not welcome the divorce and understandably did not want to uproot themselves from one home that was familiar to a home that was less so. The visits made the divorce real. And although they loved their father, they wished with all their hearts that they didn't have to go. What they wanted was for Dad to come home. Unfortunately, that would not happen, and Maureen, in her attempts to comfort the kids, misunderstood them.

It wasn't the visits they disliked so much, although they found them weird and awkward—which is to be expected. It was the divorce they did not want. Maureen would comfort the kids and tell them she was sorry, that she missed them, but they had to go to Dad's. Her sincere attempts to respond to their distress only served to make them feel as if they had some power to stop the divorce and that their visits were somehow "bad" or "sad." When Maureen realized she was making her children's struggle to adjust to change more difficult by her approach to comforting, which revealed her own personal feelings about the transitions, she was able to find better ways to handle the exchange.

She recognized the need to convey not only empathy for the difficulties, but also the positives. The kids would be okay, and she would be okay during their visits. She learned the importance of being more aware of her reactions and to model healthy coping and began to project less fear and more confidence. Dad felt freer to comfort the children without the fear of supporting Maureen's initial desire to cease the overnight schedule. The children still did not like to transition, but they recognized it as the new normal and found ways to enjoy both homes after a short period of adjustment.

"Kids need their mom more."

Children learn from both parents. And they can learn different things from each parent that together create a healthy, well-balanced view of themselves, their parents, and the world around them. Yes, children need safety, attention, love, and discipline, but with the exception of safety, they can, within reason, get that in different measures from each parent.

Mothers are not more important than fathers: both are important and may play greater or lesser roles at certain stages of development. The key is for both parents to manage their own feelings, stay ready in the wings, and step up when they are needed. Our job as parents is to be a bit taken for granted, not for things always to be equal.

Early in my marriage, I complained to a close girlfriend about what I felt was a lack of my husband's responsiveness as a parent. When she asked for specifics, I rattled off a list of complaints, such as not waking up when the baby cried, not watching the baby as closely around the stairs or the kitchen, and not packing the right things for trips and outings.

Having four of her own children, she smiled and said something that I still remember today: "Give it up—he'll never be a second mommy." She was right; he is his own parent with his own strengths. Together (whether in the one home or two) we had everything we needed to raise our son well. He provided the adventure, and I provided the soft landing.

In divorce, this difference may be difficult for the more safety- or emotionally focused parent. You may envision the other parent as distant, neglectful, or unresponsive, not acknowledging the possibility that with you not present, the other can grow to fill that needed space. As parents, we have the capacity to learn and we often do, when we are forced to do so for the benefit of our children.

I'm not just saying this to be optimistic; I do realize that simple wishful thinking doesn't fix the problem. However, pessimism shouldn't be your only guide either. When you're discussing concerns or fears, focus on the facts first. If the children do not get adequate help with homework or lack good routines, discipline, or reliable transportation, it's important to discuss those issues without emotional arguments or interpreting the other parent's motivations.

A good example is that instead of saying, "The kids need to be with me during the school week because you don't make school a priority. You just think about work, not the kids," try: "I want to make sure the kids are able to have help with their homework and all the complicated school stuff during the week. I know your work schedule, and I'm concerned it's going to be difficult to find time to do both. I have my ideas, but what are you thinking would work?" You can still propose your ideas, but it is much more likely your ex will hear your concerns and have a productive negotiation that meets the needs of the kids when concerns are presented respectfully.

This approach also works for more significant concerns, such as the children being left with unsafe caretakers or alone or not monitoring them in certain situations. These issues have the best chance of resolution if they are discussed reasonably and openly. It is also possible to put some of these agreements in writing in your parenting plan (check with your attorney) to clearly document your intentions and joint responsibilities for raising your kids. It's best to address the problems rather than seek to restrict the other parent's contact.

Addressing Significant Safety Concerns

Unfortunately, there are situations for which children do need real protection, such as physical, sexual, or emotional abuse; neglect; parenting impaired by substance abuse; or severe mental health issues. However, these are the extreme, and, in most cases, there are processes in our legal system to address these concerns proactively while continuing to protect children's safety and maintain family relationships. If safety is a concern for you in any way, I strongly encourage you to address the issues with an attorney during the initial stages of your separation and divorce. But please, for your children's sake, take these steps with absolute honesty in your intention to safeguard your children and do not make the mistake of using them as a strategy to increase your power in negotiation.

Children need both of their parents—even when they are far from perfect. When children lose a parent in the midst of a divorce, it compounds their grief exponentially. I have known children who cry for their mother or father despite horrible abuse and abandonment. Most children, even older ones with highly developed cognitive skills, do not have the emotional capacity to understand the complexities of an adult's impairment or absence.

Unfortunately, in their attempts to make sense and meaning out of the difficult situation, they often integrate blame onto themselves ("I must not be good enough to be loved or for them to stay.") or onto the other parent ("It's Mom's fault; she is keeping Dad away, even though I know he wants to see me.") rather than accepting the absent parent's failings.

It is a gut-wrenching, sorrowful situation to witness. I'm not trying to dissuade those who need to protect their children from doing so—it is one of the most difficult, thankless, selfless challenges a parent must face. It makes single parenting vastly more complicated and burdensome, and

I have great respect for those who do so when it is the only safe choice. Keep in mind, however, that allowing children to have the highest level of relationship that is safe for them both emotionally and physically is the goal. If there are real safety concerns, clarify the risk with your legal support as a guide and then ask yourself and the professionals whether there are ways to eliminate the harm.

Explore supervised visits, restrictions on overnights, ongoing treatment, or other ways to hold a parent accountable for safe or sober behavior. Clarify how you and the professionals involved in the process would know when the risk is resolved—or at least minimized to the extent that less restrictions would be reasonable. It is complicated and time consuming, and you are likely to feel angry at being asked to act as a parent to your ex. You will probably need to create clear and solid boundaries that separate the children from the chaos of the ongoing legal issues and maintain respectful communication with the other parent to safeguard you and your children's peaceful daily existence. I strongly suggest good counseling support in the form of a therapist, coach, or support group. However, this is the reality for some families, and with support, good legal guidance, and a clear plan, your children can have the best possible chance for both parents to be responsibly involved in their lives.

Some Closing Guidelines

There is no way to fully capture the uniqueness of your situation and family, and I wouldn't be so disrespectful as to try, but in my experience, one thing holds true: having at least one parent who can think rationally through the difficult stuff can make a huge difference in finding workable solutions and, thus, a huge difference in the quality of children's lives during and after divorce. Of course, if your ex is a complete jerk, you being reasonable, direct, and a good listener won't make him a perfect father; however, the reverse can often be true.

If you are irrational or adversarial and tend to heighten the conflict in order to strategize, you can cause an otherwise good-enough parent to act pretty poorly. Most of us would like to think our divorce is clear cut: we are right, and if they would just listen, then the right decision could be made. What I have observed is that there are two viewpoints in every divorce that deserve to be heard. And if there are legitimate concerns, becoming locked in conflict over them tends to entrench bad will between parents and make it much worse for the kids. This is not to say you should not speak up when there is a bona fide problem. In fact, I really encourage parents to be up front early in the divorce, when they have support, rather than avoiding issues and hoping they will just go away.

Manage your emotions and remember some kid-centered guidelines that might keep you focused on the best interests of your children and avoid basing your important decisions on fear. The following are some basic reality checks:

1. **Consistency does not mean status quo. Things will change.** With divorce, there are always changes. Have a hand in making them and remember, both of you will change. He may end up being a better dad than you believe possible, and you may be a better mom than you believe. Try to envision the future in positive ways, unless you have ample evidence to the contrary.
2. **Differences are okay; he'll never be a second mom.** Kids need both parents. Whether you are a same-sex couple or a mom and a dad, both of you have plenty to teach your child. Children learn more from seeing parents work together to bridge the differences than from one "perfect" parent.
3. **His behavior as a husband does not predict the type of father he will be.** Sometimes adults' behavior in relationships is influenced by the dynamics of the relationship itself. Some parents grow when confronted with significant life circumstances or

consequences. Keep in mind that your ex may have been a crappy partner, but that does not mean he or she will be a crappy parent.

4. **Less time does not mean less of a parent and vice versa.** Parents who are divorcing often see time with children as an indication of their respective importance or value. As long as children feel that their parents are accessible and have adequate time with both parents, they don't really care about percentages. Children don't count the hours; parents shouldn't either.
5. **Money for kids (or vice versa) is damaging.** A financial settlement is separate from the parenting plan. A financial agreement is how to divide the assets acquired in the marriage; children aren't assets, things to be divided, or a parent's right. Parenting plans are agreements on how to care for the children until they are grown. The well-being of the children should be the basis for your agreements, not money.
6. **Children shouldn't make parenting decisions.** The children didn't make the decision for you to get married, and they didn't get a vote in your divorce. They have to live with the changes from the divorce, however. Hear them but don't ask them to choose schedules or allow them to decide how their relationship with either parent continues. Kids can't handle that kind of responsibility or the consequences that come with it, so don't ask them to.
7. **Your story need not be their story. Create a positive framework.** Your story of the divorce (why it happened, how it happened) is yours, not your children's. Give them the right to enjoy both parents. Encourage them to see their family history and future not as a tragic story but one with acknowledgement of the challenges and also the positive. Give your children the right to enjoy their family, no matter how unique.

CHAPTER 10 EXERCISES: MOVING FROM EMOTIONAL FOCUS TO SOLUTION-BASED FOCUS

After reading this chapter, do you recognize yourself in any of these examples? If so, consider the following and clarify your fears and need for reassurance:

1. Using the examples as a guide, describe your mind-set. What are your beliefs about your role as a parent, as well as your ex-partner's?
2. What do you fear?
3. Looking at your fears, what would you need in order to reassure your anxieties? Try to be as concrete and clear as possible. For example, do you need to see better skills, reliability, or consistency?
4. What would change, and how would this look in practice?
5. Take a look at your answers. These are the things you may wish to ask rather than focusing on your fear. How would you would feel and act differently if these changes were to take place?

As you work with your parenting partner, focus on the solutions you wish to see. Consider communicating your fears with an acknowledgement that they are how you are experiencing the situation, not necessarily the "truth" of the situation. Frame your desire for changes as a request that, if granted, would help to reassure you and reduce the level of conflict for both of you and provide a path forward. You could also acknowledge that they, too, might have fears that need reassuring and that you will consider their requests, as well. Doing so begins to focus the discussions on solving problems with a future focus rather than looking to the past for answers. It begins to build trust based on respect and, most important, creates a foundation for how to work together to meet your children's needs.

CHAPTER 11

How Divorce Actually Affects Children

AT THIS STAGE, I often offer parents a basic overview of how children are affected by their divorce/separation to help them define their concerns and separate their children's natural grief and adjustment process from actual problems and issues that need additional support to be resolved. So I offer you the following information with that same intention. I'll begin with an overview of common temporary reactions and follow with indications of more significant mental health issues that may need therapeutic support. I will also address complications, or what I think of as kids "getting stuck" in the grief process, that may be due to normal development or from (intended or unintended) adult information conveyed.

It's important to acknowledge that divorce will drastically change your children's lives, as well as your own. Their daily schedules and family relationships will change or they will at least become different in the day-to-day. Just like adults, children will experience strong emotions in divorce. However, they lack the experience and skills of adults in expressing and coping with their feelings. They need help to understand and manage the changes.

Sometimes parents can find it difficult to support their children. They become overwhelmed by fear and grief and can find themselves focusing only on the negative or ignoring any changes in their children in an attempt to avoid their own fear or guilt. By doing so, parents often miss the reality that healthy divorces can actually produce some good things for their children.

Children who have support in adjusting can develop important strengths and coping skills. Children can learn that difficult times and sad feelings are not permanent. They can develop confidence in themselves and in their family to handle challenges and create flexibility in their concepts of love, family, and commitment. Yet it is important *not* to gloss over the reality that all children will have some adjustments to the changes, and children, just like adults, will experience some level of grief and sadness. It is often hard for parents to put aside their own emotional filter and see their children's needs accurately. Parents often come together in my office with very different perspectives on how their children are coping, and these differences are often a source of ongoing conflict.

Normal Reactions to Separation and Divorce

Children's lives are changing, and their relationships and time with each parent is changing too. They will have reactions to this very real life crisis and most likely will resist the changes in some way. They may feel sad because something sad is happening in their family. They will likely have worries about the future; don't we, as well? Children are human and, just like adults, they deserve the right to grieve. Although difficult for children and parents, the following reactions can be considered normal for children during a divorce:

◊ **Irritability.** Younger and older children may have difficulty adjusting to change and may show resistance by fussiness, changes in sleeping or eating patterns, mood swings, or being argumentative or defiant.

◊ **Anger.** Children may show anger and resentment with one or both parents for disrupting their sense of normalcy. They may express anger overtly with angry outbursts, arguing, or challenging a parent's efforts to maintain established or new rules and routines.

◊ **Anxiety.** Children may have increased fears, nightmares, or anxiety regarding changes in their lives and daily routines. They may be clingy or resist separation from one or both parents, ask repeated questions about schedules, or express worry about schedule changes. Children may also occasionally experience somatic complaints, such as headaches or stomachaches.

◊ **Sadness.** Children may express sadness directly in ways such as crying or making statements that express feelings of helplessness. Older children who have learned to cover up their less socially accepted feelings might express sadness as anger or irritability.

Signs of More Serious Problems

It takes time for children to adjust to change and work through their emotional reactions. However, you should see improvement and stability over time in their moods and behaviors. If things grow worse rather than better after several months despite consistency in the new schedules and daily routines, it may be a sign that your child could need some additional support.

◊ Significant and persistent sleep problems.

◊ Persistent and frequent somatic complaints.

◊ Difficulties in ability to concentrate that have significant impact on functioning.

◊ Significant behavioral or academic issues at school.

◊ Frequent angry or violent outbursts.

◊ Refusal to participate in or lack of self-efficacy or enjoyment of previously enjoyed activities.

◊ Withdrawal from loved ones and/or peer relationships. For teens, some withdrawal from parental figures is normal, but watch for

dual withdrawal from family and peers or a change of long-term friends to new or less socially appropriate friendships.
- ◊ Drug or alcohol use or reckless behavior in older children and teens.
- ◊ Self-injury, such as cutting or eating disorders in older children and teens.

If your children are experiencing any of the more serious symptoms, take care to decrease or eliminate any conflict or schedule disruptions and, together, consider seeking professional therapeutic support for your children. Just remember you are the first line of support for your kids. Parents are the ones with the most potential for helping kids cope. Therapists are great, but they don't tuck your kids in every night and won't be there for their weddings and graduation. Seeking out help is the right thing to do if you have reason to believe you are not equipped to deal with specific issues or if you need support in helping your children adjust.

Parental Conflict and Children's Adjustment

In addition to the normal adjustment and grieving process, there may still be situations where problems that have to do with the divorce need to be addressed. There may be expected adjustment issues having to do with the practical changes in divorce, such as moving or transitioning between two homes. Children might also have bona fide complaints about the schedule or parenting of one or both parents. These issues are understandable as they adjust to new routines and relationships, and attentive, responsive parents can best help children resolve these issues. However, difficult, more emotional issues might occur, which I tend to think of as kids "getting stuck" in the normal grieving process.

Challenges can also arise due to the natural vulnerabilities inherent in childhood development. For instance, younger children are still developing cognitive and memory skills and can be easily confused by complicated schedules. Preschool and elementary school children are often naturally self-focused, imaginative, and egotistical; they can make the erroneous assumption that parents' divorce has something to do with them and imagine ways they might fix it, which can be seen as self-blame and reunification fantasies.

Middle school children and teens are busy developing their understanding of social skills, norms, and moral reasoning. They may seek adult information, take on adult issues, and be harsh in their judgments of one or both parents. This can lead to difficulties, such as expressing loyalty to one parent over the other or blaming both parents. It is also true that these entanglements can be influenced by messages from parents in distress or conflict between the parents. Complicating things even further is that kids getting stuck can often be a combination of both natural development and often-unintended messages from parents or witnessing parents' ongoing conflict.

If parents do suspect their children are having ongoing difficulties—whether simple adjustment issues or deeper emotional challenges—the trick is not to rush to assumptions and blame or veer into fear, hopelessness, or anger. Parents need to be able to step back from their own emotions and their story of the divorce and focus on solving the problem *with* the other parent rather than ignoring, blaming, or catastrophic thinking. Distinguishing between normal adjustment and serious difficulties can be challenging but doing so allows parents to intervene with appropriate strategies that will help their children cope better.

Three months into their separation, John and Maggie disagreed bitterly about their four-year-old child's adjustment. Maggie described his uncontrollable tantrums and believed that the stress of Dad's absence caused these behavioral outbursts. John, however, saw the same behavior as a normal part of their child's development. What was clear to me—and unclear to them—was that although they were both partly right, they were, in fact, embroiled in an adult argument wrapped in a child problem.

Maggie had expressed on many occasions that John seemed to lack awareness and empathy for the profound changes that the divorce had brought to her and their child. Meanwhile, John had voiced frequent frustration at what he saw as Maggie's continual tendency to focus on the negative. How they viewed their child was impeded by their own emotional processes in the divorce.

Sometimes it is important to know the underlying reason why a child is behaving in a certain way, and sometimes it is less so. For this child, it was important that Mom was reluctant to provide control for the tantrums because she felt guilty about disciplining what she thought was the child's grief. And Dad responded by ignoring or dealing harshly without comfort to the tantrums, also out of guilt and a fear that if he responded, he was giving credence to Maggie's concerns. The end result was that their four-year old was becoming more and more out of control and not getting consistent support for his behavior and emotions. I suggested that, although they disagreed on the origin, they could both respond to their child with what he needed in the same way by addressing the behavior within good boundaries. They could respond to the emotion with comfort. And if that was not successful, they could look deeper for understanding to come up with new strategies. They found that dealing with the problem, rather than arguing about the blame, was more productive and ultimately met their child's needs.

CHAPTER 11 EXERCISES: SUPPORTING YOUR CHILDREN IN DIVORCE

Take a few moments to think about your relationship with the other parent and imagine how this relationship is likely to play out in the future if the situation remains the same. Put your children forefront in your mind and ask yourself how they would likely experience daily life in the context of this relationship. If they are too young to understand their experience, imagine them at an older age with the ability to share their feelings and thoughts more clearly and then answer the following questions:

1. How would they generally describe your relationship?
2. How would they describe the way in which you both make decisions for them?
3. How might they describe your feelings and behaviors toward their other parent?
4. How might they describe the other parent's feelings and behavior toward you?
5. Could you foresee any consequences of your current relationship for your children, positive or negative?
6. Is there anything you'd like to see change between you and the other parent to help your children feel supported in their childhood?
7. If there are things you'd like to see change, how might you accomplish those goals (e.g., personal changes or support such as a therapist or co-parent counselor)?
8. Do you foresee your children needing support above and beyond what you and your ex can provide? If so, why? For example, do your children have any specific or special needs, such as anxiety or depression or learning issues?

After answering these questions, if you have parenting relationship issues around your children's specific or special-needs issues, you may wish to take a look at this book's Resources section for some guidance in finding additional support. But remember: unless children have specific or special needs, parenting issues come first. Children should not be asked to solve or unnecessarily cope with adult issues.

CHAPTER 12

How to Make Good Decisions at the Worst Time

THE BIGGEST IRONY is that divorce forces you to make important decisions with long-lasting consequences at the absolute worst time. The discussions can often begin while still living together as you attempt to uncouple while still navigating the complexities and ongoing responsibilities of family life. You are likely swamped with difficult emotions, such as longing, fear, sadness, and anger; you are often overwhelmed, tired, and confused. Still, the decisions need to be made, and it may feel like an in-between world of what used to be and what will be.

You may feel torn between either having to trust your soon-to-be-ex when, presently, there is very little trust *or* gathering an arsenal to create a strategy for fighting the person you once loved. The idea that these are the only two choices is all too common in divorce, and that often sets the stage for ongoing hurt, chaos, and conflict. I believe there is another way, and I hope, through my experience, you can see a middle ground: a nonaggressive and a respectful but assertive course.

Deciding Who Deserves What

When I first began this journey, I received all sorts of well-intentioned advice from friends and family that centered on what I "deserved." Many argued that *he* should "pay" for his decision to leave—that any sympathy for him was misguided and an indication that I was still in denial about my marriage ending. They claimed he was untrustworthy and did not care about me or my future but only about himself. However, such talk only stoked the fire of my need to protect myself, and it was in this mind-set that I began my divorce.

Although I was cooperative and even-keeled about most day-to-day decisions, anything that indicated change triggered a response that translated into "Your decision—you suffer." Part of me believed that if my husband wanted to leave, he deserved the negative consequences. The other part did not want to participate in anything that ended my marriage, because, somehow, that meant accepting defeat. However, I was finally forced to realize that the divorce was going to happen whether I wanted it or not. Sitting in front of two lawyers can bring that home quite sharply. Decisions were being made about my life and my son's life, and in my checked-out and/or combative state, I was not participating in the decision making or creating my own future.

While we all have the right to our feelings, when it comes time to make important decisions, try not to make them from that emotional place. Anger, sadness, denial, and fear are not good or reliable vantage points from which to plan your future. Most people, when faced with a divorce that was not their idea, think about "what I deserve" or "what I can get" rather than "What do I need?" This is partly due to fear of the future but also how our legal system is structured regarding family law.

Now, I am no lawyer, but I have learned—from my own experience in the legal process—that divorce follows the same process that guides attorneys in other areas of law, such as civil and criminal, and it has a lot to do with precedents. Even though few divorces actually end up in court, precedents indicate what other courts have decided in the past. They provide some insight into determining what people can reasonably expect to get (or have to give up) in their particular case.

Based on that standard, each partner makes "offers" that are negotiated, and both parties try to retain the most (and lose the least) from the agreement as possible. This approach works great for people who will never have to lay eyes on each other again, but it can be detrimental for families that need to maintain long-term responsibilities to each other and their children. So what's the answer?

I believe that working in collaborative law, which is based on clarifying and communicating what each person needs (including parents determining their children's needs), leads to a much better relationship and more durable agreements than simply asking, "What can I get?" This concept was a starting point from which I could advocate for myself, create my own future, and be assertive rather than aggressive (or passive-aggressive, as was often the case). I began looking forward rather than backward. I discuss collaborative law as a viable option in detail in a later chapter.

But I can hear you protesting, "What if the other person won't play nice? Won't I get screwed?" I'm not suggesting that you be unrealistic about how best to protect yourself, but regardless of your partner's views, you can at least clarify for yourself what *you* need and why. You may choose to share that with your partner or not, but knowing what is essential to your well-being can help you make decisions from a rational, long-term perspective rather than from an emotional and reactionary place.

While I am not a legal professional, a note of caution is prudent: Before sharing information with your partner, it is a good idea to run it by your attorney. There are different levels of information sharing for different divorce processes, and you should be in harmony with what your attorney thinks is best. If your attorney advises you not to share, keep in mind that it is your family, and you have the right and (I believe) the responsibility to manage your attorney's approach to representing you.

For example, I vehemently protested keeping the marital bed. I took a principled stand that I could not live with the memories I felt were stored in that piece of furniture. I didn't care that it hurt his back or was the most expensive piece of furniture we had: I dug in my heels. Looking back, not taking the bed was more about hurting my soon-to-be ex. I wanted him, literally, to sleep in the bed he had made.

At some point, though, I became a bit more realistic and accepted the bed, and I can tell you it's one of my favorite things; I now look back on my temporary stubbornness with chagrin. Knowing what you need will help you to pick your battles and guide your decisions to the outcomes you most value. You will know when to take a stand and when to let it go. If you can both come from a place of what you need rather than want or deserve, it often leads to the best outcomes.

Difference Between Interests and Positions

The first step to defining your needs is distinguishing between your "interests" (what you really want) and your "positions" (the solutions *you* believe will get you what you want). Begin by being realistic about what a "good outcome" looks like or at least what you can live with and still have the future you want/need. Be as detailed as you can. Rather than "I want to be the primary parent" or "I want the house," ask yourself what those things would give you.

As an example, "I want our kids to have a parent primarily focused on them until they are in school." Another could be, "I want the kids to have the consistency of the home they grew up in," or "I want to live in a house not an apartment." You can keep digging deeper into what is truly important until you get a full picture of *why* you want certain things. Your ideas are not "right," nor is anything contradicting them "wrong"; they are simply a place to start from that represents your authentic wants.

Your partner may also have similar or conflicting wants. If you feel it is safe to do so, it's helpful to learn why your partner wants certain things. Try to really hear them articulate their version of a future so you can begin to see what is possible. Then you'll know which conflicts will need to be resolved.

"Winning" Is Not the Goal

The goal of advocating for your wants and needs in divorce negotiation is neither to "win" nor allow your partner to dictate the terms of your future life. What you'll hope to create is "a fair and durable agreement." This family law term means that you both agree to what serves each of you now and long into the future. You may not get everything you want, nor will your partner, yet you'll both be able and willing to fulfill the agreements made.

This is so important because these agreements are not the end, especially if you have children. The financial and parenting agreements are the legal blueprints for how to move forward. They are the rules and the guidelines that will direct your assumptions about the future and specify your day-to-day rights and responsibilities. If one or both partners feel they have "won" or "been taken to the cleaners," it paves the way for resistance, misunderstandings, outright conflict, and potential future litigation, which may threaten to undermine your children and your family's ability to adjust to the new life you want to build.

I can completely understand feeling that you got "screwed" out of your old dreams, but is that really a reason to screw up your—and possibly your kids'—new dreams? One thing I've learned is that it's a hell of a lot better to make good with what you have rather than focus on what you've lost. So focus on the areas in which you can still work reasonably with your ex and make the most of them. If you have some financial assets, healthy kids, a good education, a sustainable job, good friends, a place to live—you get the idea—then build on those things. Even if your soon-to-be ex is not playing fair, you still have the power to choose your own path forward, so make it one you can live with and that reflects the kind of person you are and want to be in the future.

You know the landscape better than anyone else, and it is up to you to make the best decision for yourself and your family. The following exercises can help you get started. Remember, you can share these things with your partner and/or attorney or keep them to yourself.

CHAPTER 12 EXERCISES: DIFFERENTIATING YOUR INTERESTS FROM YOUR POSITIONS

This exercise can help you clarify your interests, meaning the things you want to see happen during the divorce process and as an outcome of the decisions you make. Take a moment to write a few needs or wants for the following sections. Some may have more needs/wants than others.

1. Find some quiet time to think about what a positive future would look like, one that accepts the reality of the changes that divorce will bring. You may want to think in images, such as your child's sports events. Or pretend you are looking around at your future home or imagine a conversation with your now-ex about finances or children.
2. List what you feel you need or want for yourself as a parent or individual during and after the divorce.
3. List your most important hopes/goals for your child(ren) that you want to see during and after the divorce.
4. List your hopes or wants for your child(ren)'s other parent during and after the divorce.
5. List what you most want to see for your family during and after the divorce process.
6. For each item in each section, take some time to write a few sentences, a list, or a paragraph to describe as fully as you can why you feel this way or what this want/need, if granted, would help you attain.

This is your mission statement and can serve as a guide as you move through the divorce process and help keep you focused on positive future goals during challenging times.

CHAPTER 13

The Adjustment to Head of Household

YOU MAY BE SEPARATED or began living in different homes before or sometime during the divorce, but however it happened, as you've probably discovered, living alone can be a huge shift. It makes things real for you, and if you have children, for your kids. It's a new beginning, and it also marks an end of your life as it once was and will never be again. Yet it's the little things that can get to you.

As one child put it poignantly, "It's when I set the table and there are only three places instead of four—that's when I remember everything has changed." Whether you remain in the family home or move into a new place, both have their challenges and benefits. Knowing what to expect can be helpful so you know you are on the right path; you are not the only one who has felt this way, and this is a temporary adjustment. Home *will* feel like home again at some point.

If you have stayed in the family home, it can feel mighty empty. Things that you were accustomed to are missing; a person is missing, and you and your children will most likely feel the absence. It can feel overwhelming and lonely at times. The bed is now your bed, not "ours." If the dishwasher breaks, it's you who has to fix it. There are ghosts in the house, memories of different times that were shared, and in each room, in different moments that can visit you with a melancholy presence.

However, there are good things too. That couch you hated—gone. There's the clutter you get to clean up without someone accusing you of moving things where they can't be found. You can decide who is welcome or not welcome. You can develop your own style rather than blending yours to make both of you happy. This is your space, your furniture, and your future.

If you have moved to a new home, you may miss the familiar. If your former partner continues to live in the family residence, you may feel like you want to "go home" but cannot. It can make you feel uprooted and homesick. Your children may wonder why you can't go home, as well, and why they can't just pop over to Dad's and grab their missing socks, or why you can't just stay a bit and hang out while you're dropping them off. Your stuff is there and your memories too. You have to buy a new can opener. You have to make a home and new memories in a place that has no history.

You must struggle to fill this blank canvas, when all you want to do is reclaim the past picture of your life. Still, too, your new home is a place for you to create yourself and envision your own future. You may decide to recreate old family traditions or start new ones to fit your new vision of the future. It's exciting and scary and a bit sad too.

With your new home, whether staying put or finding new digs, there are new opportunities but also new responsibilities. Identifying those challenges clearly can help you to be ready for the tasks ahead, to focus your energy on acquiring skills and solving the problems rather than becoming fearful and disheartened. If you can see these issues as a normal part of the adjustment to your new independent life that can be met successfully rather than viewing them as overwhelming obstacles, you are much more likely to move through this time with a growing confidence and pride. You can feel that, regardless of what life has dealt you, you (and your children) can not only survive but thrive.

The new responsibilities that you will most likely have to face include taking care of a home solo: cooking, shopping, cleaning, yard work, and repairs are no longer shared. Learning to manage your finances, if that was not something you took care of previously, will also be a part of the bargain. If you have children, you will be the parent on duty and won't have backup or be able to "tag team" when things get difficult or if you have more than one child. It's hard. I know.

However, remember my suggestion that your ex may be a better ______ than you believed? It's true, and you get to fill in that blank when it comes to yourself, as well. You can become great at managing finances, create a new career, or get more focused and energized at work. You can become a whiz at organizing the home or creative landscaping. You can create great routines, discipline, and fun for the kids. This is the time to explore and to test your limits. The trick is to see this as a chance to grow your skills, to give yourself permission to do things less than perfectly, and to try rather than worry about making mistakes. It's a time for humor and humility.

Being a single mom to a three-year-old was challenging, to say the least. The difficult phases seemed to last forever, and they came in waves. As soon as the naps stopped, refusing to go to bed began, and the tantrums of an exhausted little boy frustrated every evening task. One night in particular stood out. It was after 10:00 p.m.; our bedtime routine had started three hours earlier, and still no sleep. I began with back-tickles, bedtime stories, and songs and ended with threats to take away blankie, stuffies, and Thomas trains. I tried reason that degraded into emotional pleas.

When I found myself in the kitchen with a floor full of Thomas trains and my son throwing more out every few moments, I realized that whatever I was trying was failing. In that moment my anger, sadness, and fear about my ex and the divorce hit me full force. I stood in that kitchen and sobbed. After some time, when I dared to hope he was finally asleep, four little fingers appeared beneath the door and pushed yet another train into the hall. I surprisingly broke out in laughter. The situation was absurd but it was also pretty damn funny. It was just one night and one bad “mommy moment,” as I called it; all I knew was that I needed to take a different path.

I took a deep breath, opened the door, and announced that we were going to have a “do-over.” I opened my arms and my boy snuggled in. We took a look at the kitchen and laughed. I laid him down and explained that we would be okay, and he fell asleep in my arms. In that moment I realized it doesn't have to be perfect. It just has to end with getting done what needs to be done and with him going to sleep knowing he is loved and safe. That was when I found my own voice, my own path as a single mom. And you will find your own—maybe after a bit of struggle, but you will find it. As in any journey, the first step is mapping out the path and getting an idea of the landscape ahead of you.

Remember, this is a time for moving forward, creating new possibilities for yourself, and having a willingness to make a bit of a mess since no one is looking over your shoulder. You no longer have to do things to meet another person's expectations—your standards are the only thing that matters. It can be scary, but it can also be quite liberating. Here's an exercise that can help to clarify your strengths and identify what roles/tasks you might have to grow into.

CHAPTER 13 EXERCISE: MARRIED VERSUS SINGLE-PARENTING ROLES

Think for a moment about your marriage. What roles did you and your ex-spouse provide? You may want to break them out into broad categories, such as primary caregiver, household, finances, or travel planner, and make one set of answers for each if that helps you to get more detailed information.

1. Which roles and tasks did you take care of and consider your strengths?
2. Has divorce resulted in you losing or changing any of those roles?
3. Has divorce caused you to have to take on any new roles/tasks?
4. Are any of those new roles a challenge or a stretch for you?
5. How exactly are they challenging? Be as specific as you can (e.g., lack of knowledge, emotions, lack of resources for help).
6. What concrete steps can you take to meet these goals? Create at least one bold step for each challenge (e.g., read a book, ask for help, create a spreadsheet).

CHAPTER 14

Adjustment to Single Parenting

THE BIGGEST RESPONSIBILITY for divorcing parents with children is how to not only help the children cope with the initial crisis but also how to continue raising good, resilient, healthy kids far into the future. As I described, being a single parent is not without its frustrations and anxieties. Reading parenting books can give you some great strategies and ideas, but if you aren't in the right mind-set or are filled with anxiety, guilt, or sadness, they can also end up making you feel overwhelmed and confused rather than motivated and confident. I do heartily suggest you read books about co-parenting in divorce, though. Some of my favorites are listed in the Resources section of this book. But here I'm focusing on some basic principles to help you to create an approach that fits with your parenting style and meets the most fundamental areas of support your kids need.

Being a Single Parent in a Two-Home Family

The biggest factors to help kids adjust to a separation and/or divorce and find stability in a two-home family are freedom from parental conflict and supportive, effective parenting during and after divorce. Avoiding conflict is multifaceted: it means not only that children do not witness actual arguments between parents but also that conflict, seen or unseen, does not interfere with their ability to get their daily needs met or negatively affect their relationships with one or both parents.

Conflict can be insidious, though, and affect your children deeply, even if they never witness you fighting or hear you utter a negative word. It is in your body language, the way you react when they share information about the other parent, or complete silence and refusal to speak about the other parent. One mother stated proudly, "I never have conflict with her father; I just pretend he doesn't exist." What this mother failed to understand is that the father was a very important part of her daughter's life, and she felt a need to protect her mother by living two separate lives and keeping her life with Dad a secret.

Another child explained how his parents' refusal to talk to one another affected his ability to carry on with his social and school activities: "If I want something, I have to ask Mom, and then I have to ask Dad the same thing. They won't talk, and I can't even be sure if I'm going to get a ride to practice or who is going to pick me up. Their problems are screwing everything up for me." Hopefully, major child-related issues were dealt with directly during the divorce period, so it is up to both of you to continue that process. However, if conflict ran through your divorce unimpeded and you are only now acknowledging the difficulties, it's time to start dealing.

Conflict Resolution Techniques

The most important role of the parenting plan is to clarify roles and responsibilities in order to alleviate conflict. Sure, you can deviate from the plan if both of you agree to, but if not, it is your blueprint for how to operate efficiently and successfully as parents. Still, there will be things to discuss. The techniques are the same as during divorce: acknowledge your own needs, feelings, and wants directly and respectfully and then ask the same of your parenting partner. The following are some tips on how to make those discussions more productive:

Step 1: Each parent should commit to shielding the children from conflict.

It can be in a written document or a verbal agreement, but both parents should acknowledge the damage their fighting imposes on the children and do what is in their power to keep kids from witnessing conflict. Commitment means protecting children from witnessing actual arguments, but it also includes managing conflict in ways that will not interfere with the ability to make parenting decisions or children's ability to enjoy their time and build positive relationships with both parents.

Step 2: Create boundaries between child issues and adult issues.

Separate other legal issues and create a sanctuary for parenting discussions. Create a structure for how to communicate. It can be a regularly scheduled weekly email, phone call, or face-to-face discussion, and you can agree on what information to share. While that may seem overly formal, it can help protect the needed flow of information during high-conflict times. Agree not to discuss child-rearing issues at other times, such as transitions or when the children are present.

Step 3: Discussions ~~may~~ will get emotional.

Establishing some basic ground rules will help each of you manage the inherent conflict and do the best thing for your children. The following are some good ones to consider:

Create a signal to stop escalating conflict.

It can be a hand signal or a word, but it should mean you both stop talking without exception. After a five-minute break, you both decide whether you can be calm enough to continue or should postpone the discussion for another time or place. Note that if and when you do continue, start from the beginning rather than continuing the argument from where you left off.

Stick to describing behaviors rather than making interpretations.
Don't assume you know why your ex is behaving in a certain way. Instead, describe the behavior; state your concern, as well as the effect it has on you and/or the children; and offer a possible solution. For instance, rather than saying, "You're always late picking up the kids—you don't make the kids a priority and make them sit and wonder if you'll come at all," try: "I'm noticing that you are often fifteen to twenty minutes late. I try to get the kids ready on time, but that leaves them waiting and asking if you are coming. I think they are anxious. I'm wondering if moving the time a half hour later would be better, or do you have another idea?"

Focus on problems that need to be resolved.
You will both parent differently, and every perceived "problem" does not need a solution. Children adjust better to differences than they do to conflict.

Be respectful.
Listen as well as speak. When you are not in agreement, challenge yourself to hear to the other's point of view—not for agreement, but to understand the other's perspective. Stay engaged and ask for a break if you begin to get overwhelmed or shut down. Most importantly, if you hurt the person, apologize. Just as conflict generates more conflict, goodwill generates a foundation of respect that can help to build a more positive parenting relationship.

Most likely you will have some success and many failures. You may find you need additional support from others, such as a divorce coach, therapist, or mediator. However, making a sincere attempt is building a respectful foundation for your parenting relationship and putting into action your commitment to protect your children's childhood.

What if, however, the real issue is how you each parent your children or you want to establish consistency despite differences in your home life and parenting styles?

How Children Experience Parenting Differences

There will most likely be big and small differences in your parenting styles and the choices you each make. You probably saw these differences in your marriage but worked hard to come to agreement. With the end of the marriage each parent has more freedom to develop their own style and create their own day-to-day routines. This means that your differences might become much more apparent and can give rise to the idea that one parent is "better," meaning more skilled or committed than the other. Or that one person should change their practices to fit in with the other parent's to provide consistency for the children.

Obviously, this is a big issue and can lead to a lot of conflict, which leads me to explain how *kids* experience the differences, what they essentially need in both homes, and how parents can bridge their differences and minimize conflict.

The first thing to consider is that each parent has the primary responsibility to care for the children during their residential times. By virtue of divorce, they have the right to parent in their own way as long as it meets the kids' needs for physical and emotional safety and their school, social, and relationship needs. One parent should not undermine the other parent's role and equal importance as a parent. That means that there can be differences, and, as I stated earlier, we all have our strengths and weaknesses.

Does it help if the kids have some basic rules that overlap each home and teach shared values? Of course. But fighting about establishing these rules, if both are not in agreement, is most likely going to cause greater harm than the benefits that consistency would offer. It's really a matter of, again, picking your battles. Does it matter if your child does not get their insulin shots regularly in the other parent's home? Absolutely, and it would definitely be considered a safety issue. However, if one home is not buying organic or a certain brand of cereal for breakfast, it's not a critical issue, but it could be mentioned as a concern. It is still up to the other parent to decide whether they will act on it or not. One parent cannot control the other's parenting on nonessential matters.

Information sharing is great if it works, but no one wants their ex as a parenting cop overseeing their daily routines. When in doubt, butt out. If not a serious issue, you may simply want to help children understand and respect the differences but support them in following the rules in each of their homes. Better yet, work on creating a relationship with your ex where it is safe to share advice and information without fear of being criticized or forced to take that advice. Ultimately, your power lies in the structure, schedules, and rules that you create in your own home. Focus on your own parenting and home life rather than trying to exert control over your former spouse.

Rosa was an excellent mother to her three boys both before and after the divorce. However, her well-honed ability to schedule activities, organize homework, and arrange social events made her fearful of stepping back and allowing Dad to take over any of these responsibilities, even though it was necessary for him to establish competence in taking care of these important needs.

At every transition, she sent Thomas an exhaustive list of everything to remember and how to accomplish each and every task, ad nauseam. Rosa could not understand why her ex didn't appreciate her attempts to "help." When Thomas finally shared that he felt controlled and micromanaged, she understood in principle but could not keep from continually giving advice. Rosa was frightened that her boys' lives would fall apart without her, that they would be confused and Dad would not maintain her standards.

Thomas, in turn, was paralyzed by the constant scrutiny. He hesitated to share any mishaps or ask for any information. The boys' offhand conversations with Rosa unintentionally set off a firestorm of concerns that were then relayed to Dad, and so on. With the help of their divorce coach, Dad finally was able to acknowledge Rosa's fears yet set some firm boundaries about his right to parent and make some mistakes while learning new skills. Rosa was able to see this as a more normal part of Dad's adjustment rather than evidence of his incapability. Dad did take some of Mom's advice, but also threw in a few of his own strategies and routines; despite the differences, the kids maintained their school success and participation in their social activities.

Many times, it's the adult emotions that add to conflict around parenting. A conversation about braces care can be a conflict over the perceived level of priority or commitment the other has about the children's well-being or about the financial struggles in disguise. Often, "themes" show themselves over several different situations, and you may notice yourself or your parenting partner having intense reactions that are unexpected. Take a moment to see if this might be true in your interactions with your ex or in the interactions with your kids that cause you to think negatively about the other parent.

CHAPTER 14 EXERCISES: IDENTIFYING SOURCES OF CONFLICT

Take few deep breaths and think about your recent interactions with your children's other parent, then answer the following:

1. Does emotion challenge your interactions with the other parent? When and in what situations?
2. Think of an instance in which your emotions were very strong or unexpected. Really try and feel it deeply and strongly.

3. Regarding the instance in #2, what emotions did you feel? List them.
4. What thoughts did you have that related to these feelings? Write them down.
5. Pause and ask yourself, based on your feelings and thoughts, what you needed at that time. Some common needs are:
    - ◊ To be "seen" or felt (validation)
    - ◊ To be understood
    - ◊ To be respected
    - ◊ To be supported (help!)
6. Ask yourself whether this is something that you can reasonably expect from the other parent.
7. How have you typically asked for this need to be met from the other parent? (Directly or indirectly? Using emotion or using reason? Respectfully or provocatively?)
8. If you do need or still want this from the other parent, what might you do or say to be better heard and increase your chances of getting what you want?
9. Ask yourself if there is anything you can do to meet this need yourself or apart from your ex? From whom? How?
10. Knowing this, will this strategy work in the future to prepare for meeting this need without increasing conflict?
11. Create a plan either to change the manner in which you interact over this issue or determine how you can release yourself from looking for this reaction from your ex.
12. Take a moment to feel proud of yourself for making any small or big changes that help reduce negative interactions, help you care for yourself, and help your children's lives be more conflict free.

CHAPTER 15

Good Parenting: Establish Routines and Structure

REMEMBER THAT THE FIRST factor in helping children adjust in healthy ways during and after a divorce is conflict reduction, but good parenting is just as important. Good parenting provides the structure that allows children to feel safe in their home and know that even though some things change, their parents' commitment to raising them attentively has not changed.

Most people do not think of discipline as love, but at its core, that is exactly what motivates parents to do the hard work of watching closely, maintaining high expectations, and teaching their children with patient, loving guidance. It is also what motivates children to maintain their connection to their parents and follow their directions, despite anger, frustration, and limits on getting whatever they desire.

So what exactly is good parenting? It's not that you forget how to parent after divorce—it's just that divorce brings challenges and requires some new skills, adjustment, and lots of patience. You no longer have the other to turn to when you have reached your limit. You may be tired, afraid for yourself, and/or worried about your kids. You have the house to take care of, your finances, your own emotions to care for, and not a lot of time or energy to devote to developing parenting techniques. Yet your kids need you more—not less—during this difficult time. You can't play good cop/ bad cop or rely on someone else to create or enforce the rules when there is a lack of connection. In short, you have to do it all during your time with the kids and there is no one to fill in when you fall short. Being a single parent is a lesson in priorities: doing what is most important and forgiving yourself for not doing it all or doing it perfectly.

I would like to focus here on what your kids need most in order to feel loved, safe, and free from the chaos common in times of crisis and change. Once you get the basics, you can read, experience, experiment with new ideas, follow your own path, and create your own approach to parenting. Again, there are some good suggestions in the Resources section at the end of this book. My goal is to help you to feel effective and confident as a parent, feel freedom to enjoy your children, and begin to rebuild your sense of wholeness as a family.

Structure and Connection

Whether in divorce or in a one-home family, children need two things: structure and connection. But in divorce, they are even more important. Kids can be feeling unmoored, scared, possibly angry, and sad. Connection soothes them, reassures them they are loved and not alone in this journey. Structure reassures them that they still have leaders to guide them; it grounds them in normal life day-to-day routines. I think it's helpful to start with structure and then build in the connection, which will be discussed more fully in the following chapter. One is not more important than the other, but having a sense of peace and flow can reduce stress and make it easier to freely enjoy your children and for them to enjoy closeness with you, which is their connection.

Structure: Rules That Work

In divorce there can be a great risk of letting things go: you're tired, overwhelmed, and wanting to hunker down and take care of yourself. You may hope that the kids can give you a little space to fall apart. Instead, you're more than likely to find that they are needier, possibly testing the limits, and more emotional than ever. Parents may tend to rely on their old roles and rules and resist taking on the new more challenging ones. My suggestion is to get back in the driver's seat first, and then maybe you can put it on cruise control for a bit.

In its most simplistic form, structure means the rules, but it is also about leadership. As the only adult leader in your home now, you need to know where you are going and how you will get there to keep everyone on the same path and moving in the same direction. Rules fall into two main categories:

◊ rules that get the needed tasks done, and
◊ rules that teach each child skills for independence and successful relationships.

They certainly can overlap, but it's helpful to break them into categories in order to get some clarity.

Rules for Getting Things Done: Routines

Routines help your home run smoothly. Each member of the family is asked to do their part, which keeps the leader from becoming overwhelmed by doing every task. For younger children, this can mean taking care of themselves in smaller ways, such as morning routines of getting ready with clothes and brushing teeth while you make breakfast. For older children, it can mean taking care of themselves but also doing their part for the family, such as age-appropriate chores.

Having these tasks laid out in a clear routine helps everyone know what is expected of them; they might need reminders or assistance. A self-sustaining flow of routine avoids expending unneeded energy, helps each member feel successful and needed, and most important, creates peace and space for fun.

Rules for Independence and Successful Relationships

Our job as parents is to teach our children how to become successful, independent human beings. Discipline is simply setting the expectations for their learning and the conditions for success, as well as monitoring and motivating their progress. It's not always fun or enjoyable, but if you can develop a mind-set that you are doing a loving and necessary job for the good of your children, it can be a lot easier.

One thing that I find really important (and something a lot of parents skip) is being clear and thoughtful about the rationale for the rules you want your child to follow. It's important for two reasons:

1. You are going to feel a lot more confident knowing that what you are doing is a good thing for your child, and
2. Your child is much more likely to see your actions as loving and understandable if they know what they are learning and why—but don't expect to be thanked.

When I tell my son he cannot have unlimited video games, he knows why: because I want him to enjoy all the other great things out there for him and so he doesn't become one of those adult gamers who lives alone in an apartment filled with empty Big-Gulp cups (okay, so I don't tell him the last part). I sometimes say no to buying a Lego set because I want him to learn how to still be happy without getting everything he thinks he wants. Your kids may need to learn that badgering and whining leads to "NO" so they can learn that not always getting their way is normal and that it annoys friends and other important people in their lives (including you). There are plenty of other examples if you stop and think about how your rules can teach important life lessons.

While setting rules and explaining the reasons behind them is great, also plan for the consequences when they do not heed your wise advice. Parents know that children misbehave or ignore or defy the rules, yet many neglect to set out their strategy proactively, before they need it. Then, when faced with the inevitable challenge, they are caught unprepared. Sometimes parents think that if their kids respected them, they would follow the rules, and therefore they interpret children's misbehavior as a challenge to their authority. So they attempt even more control, which typically backfires. Conversely, they may feel their relationship is threatened when their kids need consequences and seek to bridge the gap with even more closeness.

These are both understandable reactions, especially if your relationship with your kids is still operating on the assumptions and roles of parenting with a partner. The danger, however, is that when your strategy fails to get the desired response, you may become frustrated, unsure, and, seeking to protect yourself and your kids from the hurt or anger, begin to withdraw your love or your guidance or both. The trick is to expect children to fail in kid-like ways. Do not take it as a parenting or personal failing; simply allow the consequence (hopefully fair, reasonable, and logical) to do its job.

CHAPTER 15 EXERCISES: CREATING SUCCESSFUL ROUTINES

If you notice certain times of the day or week are consistently stressful or chaotic, then you may wish to take some time to develop a clearer routine. Typically, parents find these "pinch times" arise during peak busy times: mornings, after school, and evenings. Use this exercise if you feel the need to create a better family "flow" by answering the following questions:

1. Are there any consistently challenging times or issues in your daily routine? List these times.

2. Choose one at a time and answer the following:

    a. List the important tasks/activities that need to be accomplished during this time on a separate piece of paper, if needed.

	Time	Kid tasks	Parent tasks/activities
1.			
2.			
3.			
Etc.			

    b. What about this schedule isn't working as well as you'd like? Circle the problem areas and list the issues that could arise.

    c. What do you want to see instead? What are the goals, or how do you envision this time successfully?

    d. Ask yourself what issues might arise? Some common challenges:

        ◊ Designating too little time.

        ◊ Trying to multitask unsuccessfully.

        ◊ Trying to fit something in that doesn't work well.

        ◊ Expecting children to independently manage their behavior or task without direction, monitoring, reminders, or training for independence.

        ◊ Not planning ahead.

e. How might this schedule work better? On a separate piece of paper if needed, list what would success look like.

	Time	Kid tasks	Parent tasks/activities
1.			
2.			
3.			
Etc.			

3. What changes will you have to make to support success with the new schedule? Some common approaches include:

◊ Rearrange or streamline the schedule; let go of what's not working.

◊ Start earlier or shorten/lengthen time needed for completing tasks.

◊ Readjust your expectations for the kids' behavior and increase assistance, monitoring, direction, and reminders (written or verbal). Create a behavior plan/instructions for the kids to help them manage their tasks independently.

◊ Plan ahead and prepare (e.g., make lunches the night before).

4. Clearly inform each of the family members of their tasks for each routine.

◊ Create a list of what they are expected to do and when, then post it somewhere visible.

◊ For younger children, you may want to break the tasks into smaller steps and add pictures to help guide them.

◊ Remember that it is normal to assist, monitor, or remind kids in order to help them become independent in their tasks. This is true even for older children.

CHAPTER 16

Creating Connection

CHILDHOOD SHOULD be a safe container, but not completely comfortable. Instead of children experiencing the massive consequences of adult life, they should have the opportunity to experience smaller consequences they can learn from. I like to think of this as letting a kid fall off the curb instead of the cliff or like getting a bad grade rather than flunking out of college. Parents who provide and allow for these lessons balance protecting their kids as children and preparing them for successful independent life.

However, instead of telling you which techniques to use, I simply want to help you create an open mind-set: to motivate you to seek out the information you need and feel good about trying new things as a parent. Even as a child specialist, I don't use every good idea myself; I just try to enjoy the good stuff and keep my eye on proactively addressing routines and behaviors that need attention. I try to stay on my toes, but I'm not always perfect, and you won't be either.

Connection Building

One of the important ways connection happens is through shared meaning about the history of your family, the challenges of the changes you are experiencing, and your hopes and dreams for your future. This can be difficult for parents who may have their own ideas about the marriage and divorce and struggle with how to appropriately explain a dark period in their family's lives. Parents begin creating this meaning and building their children's framework of understanding when they first disclose the impending divorce. The "divorce talk" sets the tone and expectations for the kids to build on as they go through the process. How that was done tells children a lot about the meaning of the divorce itself. If only one parent did the talking while the other silently cried or fumed, that tells them something. Conversely, if both parents spoke openly and reassured them of their commitment to parenting and their confidence that everyone in the family would be okay, that tells them something quite different.

Children need to know the basics: what is happening, why (without judging or blaming one or both parents), how it will happen, and when. Knowing this helps prepare children for the upcoming changes and reassures them of their parents' willingness and ability to lead. It sets the stage for developing a more positive, resilient story of family rather than an out-of-the-blue tragedy.

Love and Connection

Love and enjoyment of each other is the bedrock of family. It's why we do what we do and the end goal of all of our hard work. Providing rules and structure serves to maximize close times by minimizing conflict. The less time you need to spend on discipline, the more time there is for fun. However, solo parenting often means you have little time for spontaneous moments; there are double the tasks to do in the same amount of time. You may feel guilty when your child asks to play and you know dinner needs to be started. You may feel exhausted and just want to check out when your child makes yet another bid for your attention.

Have Fun

One of the ways to find time for closeness is first to acknowledge to yourself and possibly to your kids that you have less energy for closeness but that doesn't mean you care less. Don't waste precious time feeling guilty. Attempt to build connection into everyday routines: focus on being present and attentive for short periods and utilize teachable moments (discipline) as ways to connect deeply.

Creating new rituals is another way to ensure togetherness and encourage interaction in your daily routines. Try a regular game night or use dinnertime as a fun way to reconnect. Some ideas could be taking turns describing the best and worst part of the day or playing a guessing game (e.g. "What's my favorite color?"). You could also find ways to use children's discussions of daily life as a way to open up more about you. Kids like to know about their parents, especially stories about experiences and challenges that their parents faced when they were their age. It's important that information is appropriate and that you feel comfortable sharing, but it can go a long way to build connection, convey empathy, and have your children learn about you as a person, not just a parent.

For older kids, you can create a journal you and your child can share writing, which can make many older kids feel more comfortable. Yet another way to make time is to have a "time-in," where you set aside time to either spontaneously be present for a short period, such as playing a game, or just meeting your child's bid for attention or planning. You can also regularly set aside more extended periods (perhaps half an hour) with each child to focus only on them, give them positive feedback, and enthusiastically participate in an activity of their choice.

Discipline as Connection

Discipline can also be a time for connection. Setting limits and addressing behavior doesn't have to be harsh. You can hold your ground while maintaining connection. A hug to console a child who has lost their video time or sharing your own life lessons to soften the blow of punishment can lead to a sweet connection and confidence in your child that despite their behavior, you are still there, are still loving, and are empathetic about learning important life lessons.

CHAPTER 16 EXERCISES: CREATING A BEHAVIOR PLAN

In the busyness of parenting, kids' negative behavior often sneaks up on you. And to complicate things even more, children are constantly changing as they develop. The first part of this exercise is noticing your frustrations or worries. When you do, rather than judging yourself for the "problem" existing in the first place or not noticing it earlier, simply focus on taking steps to help your children learn to do something different. Make sure to address one specific behavior at a time and answer the following questions and prompts on separate pieces of paper or journal pages:

1. Clarify the issue.
    - ◊ What do you want your child to not do? (target)
    - ◊ What do you want them to do instead? (goal)
2. Clarify your rationale.
    - ◊ Why? How will it help your child?
    - ◊ What, as an adult, have you learned about why these behaviors are important?
3. Identify the barrier and focus on appropriate approaches.
    - ◊ Knowledge (educate)
    - ◊ Attention (give clear warning and consistent consequence)
    - ◊ Emotion/overstimulation (time-ins or time-outs)
    - ◊ Competence (seek attainable goals and manage your expectations)
    - ◊ Structure (set the conditions for them to succeed)

4. Identify your potential power for motivation: consequences.
    - ◊ What do you have control over, giving or taking away?
    - ◊ Which natural or logical consequences might be appropriate?
5. Calmly present your plan to your child. Note that a written plan can be helpful for older children. Let them know:
    - ◊ What you expect,
    - ◊ Why you expect it, and
    - ◊ The future consequences
        - * Not a discussion or argument, just the plain facts
        - * Charts that show positive progress can be motivating for younger children
        - * Praise and spontaneous gestures that celebrate success can be motivating
6. Follow through consistently.
    - ◊ Kids will test your resolve. Don't expect immediate results.
    - ◊ Welcome misbehavior as an opportunity to demonstrate follow-through.
    - ◊ Be prepared to have occasional, spontaneous "tests," even after they attain their goal and follow through as before.
    - ◊ If you find your efforts are ineffective in any way, get curious and see if you can find a possible reason, which may lead you to tweak the plan rather than give up.

CHAPTER 17

Co-Parenting with Your Ex: The Ups and Downs

SO THINGS ARE going well or at least predictably. You and your children have gotten used to your new schedule, your home is reasonably settled, and you might even be getting along with your ex pretty well at times. Things are moving along, and you think you just might be okay. Then something shifts. Maybe it's hearing your ex is dating or has a serious relationship. Or maybe it's you beginning to focus not just on survival but also on creating a new life. Whatever the cause, the old ghosts can revisit you in unexpected ways.

You might feel an intense longing for the relationship you once had, even though you thought you were over that stage. You may feel building anger that he has the funds to buy a home or take a vacation when you are still struggling to get on solid financial ground. Your car might break down and you feel a sense of abandonment as you look at your phone and try to decide whom to call. It is all part of the process.

Many times, newly single clients will ask me how long it will take them to move past these feelings. I have good news and bad news: The good news is that getting over the mountain is shorter than you think if you focus on creating stability for yourself rather than battling your ex. The bad news is that there are hills over the mountains that may stretch as far as the eye can see. It's not such a bad thing, really: slow and steady up a hill and then a nice stroll down until the next one. These hills represent the ongoing processing of the grief and loss while you're creating new dreams. Then with each new dream comes a reminder of what could have been and is not.

The first time my ex took our son on vacation to visit his family, I was struck by how that used to be my family, too, and now it was not. Standing in the driveway, I felt a sadness sneak up on me when I thought I would be reveling in some much-needed time alone. Then and there I had to decide whether I was going to feel sorry for myself and chose not to. Acknowledging your sadness and the losses is important, but think about the fact that what is an ending for you is not an ending for your child. Maybe it's just the relationship with your ex or maybe it's the ex-in-laws and the vacations, but there is no reason the children cannot enjoy these experiences and relationships fully even if you cannot.

A New Partner

One of the most common shifts happens if (or when) your ex becomes seriously involved with another partner. They may seem colder, less in contact, or more formal. You may sense your ex resisting the remaining bonds you have. Maybe you did not recognize them and only miss those bonds now that they are tested. You may find that the flexibility or the creative scheduling for kids' special events becomes more complicated or reverts to "the plan" when you never really stuck to it before.

I remember vividly when two weeks before Christmas my ex told me (I thought rather causally) over the phone that he and his partner would not be coming for Christmas dinner. We'd had that ritual since our divorce, and I unexpectedly burst into tears. I thought we were past this; we were one of the lucky families that "got along," and I was filled with panic that the comfortable relationship we had was over. It wasn't, but it did take some adjustment.

In that tense moment, my ex-husband did something very helpful and offered reassurance rather than defensiveness. He reaffirmed his commitment to our family, but he also explained we needed to make room for his new partner. She had her own desires and traditions and deserved a space to feel included. Although frightened, I could understand why she should not be expected to spend the whole of her Christmas with her partner's ex-wife. I could appreciate her graciousness for all she had already done to respect the family that came before. When my fear and grief subsided, I could view the changes in context of growing the family forward rather than focusing only on loss and my fear of change. Again, it's all about balance and working through the relationship—and you thought that ended with divorce!

Making room for another partner does not mean making you or your history disappear. It doesn't mean that when *you* get a partner that you need to erase your ex in order to show respect for the new person in your life either. You were married, you had a past, and I certainly hope your partner is aware of that fact. Still, you can do your part to make it easier. Maybe it means that you know when to take a step into the background or not share your own personal history regarding your ex too freely. Maybe it means accommodating a different view or experience that they add to your child's life. Maybe it's speaking positively about the new partner to your child and giving them permission to enjoy or even love the new person in their parent's life. I am blessed to have a great woman in my son's life; I believe she adds something invaluable to us and gives our son another model of a strong, caring woman. She also gave us a beautiful new sister (bonus!). In getting to know her, I have come to realize that, in fact, it's not easy to step into the midst of a complicated post-divorce family. I now know it doesn't in any way diminish me or my history to show some patience and empathy.

I am aware of how this all sounds—make it easier on the new partner? Why? Isn't that just taking it a bit too far? I don't think it is asking too much to give another person, who may be intimately involved in your child's life, a chance. I hope they are a good, kind, and warmhearted person. Maybe they are just neutral and you won't ever be close, but you can be cordial. Maybe they really aren't your cup of tea or they're downright nasty. The fact is you don't know until you find out firsthand.

We all come to the table filled with assumptions and are specifically primed to believe that the old partner and his or her new one are natural enemies. There are few models out there to the contrary, and we like to think of them as aberrations or out of the norm. In reality, unless your partner had an affair, the new person is completely innocent and not involved in the demise of your relationship.

If the relationship is a continuation of an affair it will certainly be much harder, but the principles remain the same. Manage your own feelings, be the adult, and base your level of interaction with them on your ability to be respectful. Above all, remember that your children will not have a choice about interacting with the person. Your approach can make it either much harder or much easier on them as they live in the world that you and your ex's divorce has created for them. Give them the freedom to make the best of the situation, be hopeful, and enjoy whatever positives they discover.

Other Triggers

Even without other relationships, there are also sneaky triggers that can get to you every time. It could be discussions about finances; differences of opinion about parenting; or just the ongoing, not-going-to-change irritation you feel about some aspect of your ex's personality or they feel about yours. The difficult truth is that you may never resolve the arguments or disagreements.

The positive side is that you don't really need to solve them. You no longer need to ask their permission about things that don't affect them personally, and they do not need to ask for yours. Sure, it's a great thing when you can listen, share, and work together for the good of the kids. I love the ability to be able to say, "Yes, of course," and give freely—but when it's not your residential time or your task, you can also say, "No thank you." That means if they suggest you only give treats on special occasion and you give one each night, you get to say, "I hear you, but I like our routine, and I'll respect yours." If it's not significantly affecting the health and well-being of your child or the other parent, then remember: when in doubt, butt out.

Co-Parenting Rules That Work

There are some good rules that I like to propose for co-parents. While there is definitely room for personalization, I have found the following rules are useful to avoid conflict and help parents work together in ways that demonstrate their commitment to their children and respect for the other parent.

1. Protect your children from witnessing conflict.

Arguments scare kids. Conflict undermines their sense that parents can take care of them. It may also make kids feel they need to take care of parents emotionally by taking sides or solving problems rather than expressing and managing their own feelings.

◊ Keep parent conversations respectful and calm when kids are present.

◊ Speak or write to each other directly and don't ask children to deliver messages verbally or carry written messages.

◊ Make transitions respectful and calm or use "natural" transitions that don't require contact, such as school/activity pickup/drop-off.

◊ Allow children to enjoy their special events by being respectful and cordial to the other parent.

2. Create clear agreements regarding responsibilities and establish regular communication.

Kids' needs don't stop in divorce; in fact, they need parents more. Parents need to find a space separate from their adult emotions and create a business-like relationship with clear roles, responsibilities, and regular communication to help children during this difficult time and beyond.

- ◊ Create good boundaries in the parenting relationship that respect each other's privacy and independence.
- ◊ Create clear agreements about parenting duties that reduce miscommunication and disagreements.
- ◊ Learn to make parenting conversations productive and take a break if conversations begin to turn into unproductive arguments.
- ◊ Create a routine of regular, clear communication of important child information.
- ◊ Communicate all the important information that enables the on-duty parent to meet kids' needs.
- ◊ Respond to communications from the other parent on a timely basis.

3. Keep adult information between the adults.

Children in divorce are living in a world of change, and they often have questions. However, questions are usually for the purpose of understanding and for reassurance rather than for information. Giving children adult information or speaking negatively about the other parent can undermine children's sense of security or give a child a sense of responsibility for managing their parents' relationship or solving adult problems.

- ◊ Offer children an accurate but developmentally appropriate and blame-free explanation for the divorce/separation.
- ◊ Keep discussions about issues in your past or present relationship with your ex child friendly; don't disclose adult information to children.

◊ Do not talk about money or child support with your children.
◊ Do not talk about disagreements in the residential schedule with your children.

4. Keep adult emotions separate from children's emotions.

Adults' needs and emotional experiences are not the same as children's in divorce. Show your children they are free to love others and that they do not need to take care of their parent's issues or emotions. Show caring by allowing children to feel supported and loved by both parents and allow them to maintain their childhood.

◊ Don't speak negatively about the other parent. Be aware that body language is just as clear as words.
◊ Speak positively about the other parent's traits, skills, or interests to your child.
◊ Give your children direct messages that you want them to have a great relationship with the other parent and repeat it often.
◊ Allow your children to enjoy their relationships with family members on both sides of the family.
◊ Allow your children to create their own relationship your ex's partner, even if it is despite your own feelings.
◊ Reassure children in words and actions that you are okay when they are not with you.

5. Keep disagreements with the other parent separate from children.

There will be disagreements, but the parents are responsible for handling disputes, not the children. Talking about adult disagreements is scary for kids. It may send a message that they have a role in solving adult problems or in managing their parents' conflict.

◊ Don't discuss issues of disagreement in ways children can become privy. If children do become aware, explain in as neutral, non-blaming terms as possible (and if able, share the incident with your co-parent).
◊ Don't attempt to take away another parent's residential time due to disagreements about money or any non-safety-related disagreements in parenting.
◊ If in conflict, make decisions about schedules that address children's needs rather than count days "owed" or given in the residential schedule.

6. Encourage children to enjoy time in both homes and share experiences.

Children in a two-home family can feel disconnected and anxious. They may have difficulty understanding the "rules" of family relationships. Parents need to actively encourage children to fully engage, enjoy each parent, and feel comfortable sharing any information they wish with either parent.

◊ Show pleasure when children share their positive stories about time with the other parent.
◊ Do not ask your children to keep secrets from the other parent.
◊ Reassure your children in words and actions that they are safe, loved, and well cared for when with the other parent.

Help Children Feel Connected with Both Parents Regardless of Schedule

Regular and consistent schedules help children and parents function well and feel connected. However, there will be times when keeping to the schedule means children would miss out on special events or contact with the other parent. From a child's perspective, schedules are their time for being loved and cared for by each parent, not a parent's right to their "time." Children are not possessions.

- ◊ Make sure both parents are free to attend children's public events (athletic games, school events, etc.) even if they occur during the other parent's residential time.
- ◊ Encourage children's interaction with both parents when they attend special events.
- ◊ Within reason, consider being flexible when needed in order for children to participate in special events or avoid long stretches without seeing the other parent.
- ◊ Make sure children have reasonable access to calling either parent when desired and not disruptive to the on-duty parent's family time.

Help Children Be Successful Managing the Challenges of Their Two-Home Families

Children's developmental tasks are harder in two-home families. Their capacity for tracking belongings, organizing time, and maintaining focus can be more challenging. Actively help your children by making rules that don't interfere with their needs and by creating age-appropriate routines and rules that make their lives easier.

- ◊ Allow children to freely take important belongings between homes.
- ◊ Help support children by creating workable routines and practices for transitioning important items between homes.
- ◊ Help support children in managing their daily life activities, such as homework, between two households.
- ◊ If possible, try to find some basic areas of agreement about discipline and routine that help children feel some continuity between the homes.

Respect Each Other's Parenting Time

Each parent is responsible for caring for children during his or her own residential time. Making plans, rules, or changes to the other parent's residential schedule without discussion and agreement can interfere with the other's ability to parent, the children's ability to adjust to and enjoy their other home, and both parents' ability to safeguard their co-parenting relationship.

◊ If children resist transition, work together to reassure them and/or address legitimate issues, if needed, rather than allow a child to refuse time with either parent.
◊ Plan non-essential or agreed upon activities for your residential time only and allow the other parent freedom to plan their own activities. If activities cross over between households, it should be by prior agreement.
◊ Don't make changes to the schedule or other agreements without directly discussing your plans and reaching agreement with the other parent.
◊ Make sure phone calls don't disrupt the other parent's time with your child; children should be offered the opportunity to make phone calls instead of rigidly scheduling calls.

Respect Each Other's Independence in Parenting

In divorce both parents need to make their homes function independently. Children should have their needs for discipline, connection, and daily life met in each home. Still, parents don't have to agree about every aspect, as long as they meet the daily and safety needs of the children.

◊ Share in the work and play of caring for the children.
◊ Create a positive plan for discipline and routines in each home.
◊ Be independently responsible for obtaining information from children's academic, recreational, and social sources.

◊ If possible, both parents should independently support their children's peer relationships by maintaining contact and engagement.
◊ Respect differences in parenting style or practices. You can discuss concerns, but if not in agreement and it is not a safety concern, it may be best to allow for differences.

Parents Should Remain the Parenting Leaders, Even with New Partners

Introducing new partners is a big transition for everyone. This can be a time of heightened anxiety, so it is not a time for making big changes to your co-parenting relationship or parenting practices. Children and the other parent will likely be sensitive and need reassurance of the family's stability and that parents will remain the leaders for all child-related issues.

◊ If possible, inform the other parent of your intention to introduce a new partner, in order to help answer questions accurately and reassure your children, if needed.
◊ Make sure parents remain the homes' leaders and make the important decisions, even if new partners become part of the family.
◊ Help your new partner become familiar with co-parenting, and support them in finding a role in the family that is respectful to them and the existing family relationships.

Things might not always go smoothly. Remember, this is a relationship with its own strengths and challenges. You may have periods when things are working smoothly, only to have an event, difficult decision, or hurt feelings bring you to the precipice where you face the urge to jump back into the angry, sad, or lonely place that you know all too well.

In that moment, the best that you can do is to recognize what is happening and take steps that bring you back from the edge. Learn how to soothe yourself and regain your balance. That could mean examining any underlying emotions or reactions that could be influencing your ability to be flexible or listen. It could mean letting go of something less than essential. It could be finding a way to explain your view that connects more and provokes less or finding some way to compromise with your parenting partner.

Remind yourself of your goal to protect the respectful relationship between you and your ex and that doing so is your loving commitment to your children in action. Maybe your parenting partner will join you in that commitment and work to make things easier; perhaps they will soften, offer an apology, listen when they disagree, or let go of their less important wants. Or maybe it will be you alone who walks the path of peace. Still, knowing that you are doing your part to protect your child from conflict is a gift not only to your child but to yourself, as well; you can find pride in the way you do the most important job you will ever have—being a parent.

CHAPTER 17 EXERCISE: PROTECTING YOUR CO-PARENTING RELATIONSHIP

Take some time to think about your co-parenting relationship and practices. Pay particular attention to how you and the other parent overlap or interact with each other in the presence of the children, how you share tasks, and how you two make decisions that affect the children. If you have not yet established your co-parenting relationship, use your imagination with this exercise to think ahead about how your co-parenting ideas might be affected by new partners in the longer-term future.

1. Are there practices that you do now with your co-parent that might be problematic with a new partner (e.g., spending holidays together or having dinners together routinely)? If so, how?

2. How do you and your co-parent make decisions or negotiate? Is it casual and spontaneous, or is it guided by established "rules"? Could this arrangement be compromised in any way if a new partner is involved? Do you assume agreement on issues that have not been explicitly discussed?
3. Are there any unspoken agreements in practices or decision making that are fine now but might be problematic if one person's situation changed (e.g., one parent consistently arranges their schedule for the other's travel)? If so, what are they?

Consider your answers for a moment and ask yourself the following questions:

1. Are there discussions that you and your parenting partner need to have about practices, communication, or casual agreements to prevent major disruptions in your life or your children's?
2. If you are not able to have these discussions right now, are there any steps you may need to take that could clarify or define accepted practices and avoid similar disruptions?
3. If need be, how might you explain these changes to your children?
4. When and how might you and your co-parent discuss the changes to be considered in a productive manner as each of your lives change?
5. How might you envision supporting new partners? What do you feel they need to know and to what extent will you be willing to change to accommodate them into the parenting and family in general?
6. What might you do if you need support either with accommodating partners or managing conflict that might result from new partners being included in the family?

CHAPTER 18

The Future You

YOU MAY HAVE reached the end of this book while you're still in the earlier stages of grief and yearn for a glimpse of what the future might hold. I get you. I spent many nights gripped with panic when considering my future. Would I every truly be okay, or would I begin my slow decline into a reality that I could not recognize and divide my life into the before and the after of divorce?

Any hopeful dreams I did possess had a *schadenfreude* quality of unmitigated triumph over my former husband. I would be more successful, more loved, fitter, and happier than he could have imagined. My dreams always centered on him: what he would think, feel, and regret. These, I know now, were fantasies that kept the fear at bay, not true dreams. In reality, I found that the true success I felt was actually centered on my growth and my strengths and not about any sort of comeuppance toward him.

Am I glad I got divorced? No. But with each passing year, I do find a more nuanced and compassionate understanding of what happened to me and how it has made our current relationship possible. I know myself now as stronger, more hopeful and positive, lighter, and more independent than I ever was before. I can also see now that I need to seek out and accept help—I need other people to make my life meaningful. I'm a better parent, a better provider, a better dreamer than I knew. Even with bad experiences, nothing is wasted.

In some aspects, I've been so lucky; in others, not so much. There will be times when I am not feeling gracious. But if I do bad, I'll apologize and fix what I can. If I do good, I'll use that lovely warm feeling to be grateful for the connections that still endure and my capacity to give what I have to offer.

It's not always equal. You may not take the same life path as your ex. A refrain you are sure to hear is: "Now you can find the real right one" or some variation on that theme. Many people believe finding a new partner will undo the loss and heal the hurt, that it's the light at the end of this dark tunnel. But it also can be a burden. If you don't find someone, does that mean you failed? No, and that's a lot of pressure, but I'm a sucker for happy endings. However, for many, it is not the "ending" that is required to feel whole and happy.

For example, you might not attain the same level of success or earning as your ex. Does that mean you have again failed? I would ask: Do you have what you need? Do you have enough to offer yourself or your children stability and joys, even if they're simple and small? If you do, then in my mind, that is enough. It isn't always fair or equal (in more things than finances), and the life you create and how it gives you joy is more important than how it stacks up against that of your ex.

My Hopes for You

Wherever you are now, I hope as you go forward you can find your own way with a seed of confidence and begin to feel a sense of solid ground under the grief. I hope you find ways to remind yourself that the hard times do not necessarily mean you are on the wrong path and remember that grief is temporary and will pass.

In the end, remember you are a powerful force in helping your kids to adjust. Use your power wisely and focus on building a peaceful, structured home that offers guidance and fun. Enjoy your kids and feel confident in your parenting, even if you fall short of perfection. If you sense a problem, face it. Read books and blogs and check in with your own sense of what feels right and what feels wrong. If it feels wrong, stop and see whether there's a better way to get the job done. If it feels right and the kids seem happy and stable, stay on your path and look to the future rather than the past. You may have a long way to go, but remember to celebrate the small things, enjoy the sweet spots, and continue to keep your eye on building on what you and your kids have, not what you have lost.

I hope that you allow yourself to dive fully into whatever happiness you create. If you have kids, I hope that your children feel the love and presence of both parents and are able to freely enjoy their childhood. I hope you find peace with your ex and new dreams for your family. I hope you can share those dreams with others who may not know that happy endings don't have to fit the formula. I truly believe—and hope that you can come to share the belief—that we, too, have a right to feel proud of our complicated, messy, not-so-traditional relationships, to enjoy the good stuff and dream new dreams for what is still family.

My Suggestions for a Great Future

As you move through this process, you will have many decisions to make and many challenges to face. While I can't anticipate them for you, I do have some general suggestions to offer that may help optimize your opportunities for growth, joy, and a sense of purpose. Even if you are lost and unsure, finding a way to make this bearable, meaningful, and, at times, finding a measure of happiness can be enough to keep you putting one foot in front of the other.

Resist Comparisons

It is understandable to judge yourself in comparison to your partner when, after all, you've been on the same journey and headed to the same destination for quite some time. You may feel he has more and you have less, or even at times vice versa. Try to remind yourself that your success is not dependent upon his failure, and, conversely, his success is not indicative of yours. This is where your paths diverge and you create your own future. Comparing yourself often just makes you feel worse, so try gently to let it go and accept that while there are changes in circumstances, you do not have to give it meaning and allow it to divert you from your path.

Focus on the Positives

There are always positives, even if they are small. Keep your eye out for whatever you can find. There are losses, but at times direct yourself to look at the spaces that have opened up for you: Are there new freedoms, new possibilities, new opportunities? Are there things that you left behind that you are actually glad to see go? It could be something as simple as not having anyone there to judge or negotiate with or simply the pleasure of solitude. It could be something as small as having the whole bed to yourself, playing your own music—loud—or something with more heft, such as parenting from your own heart and values and diving into your own dreams of career or travel. Whatever it might be, find something every day to acknowledge as good.

Create Something–Anything

You've seen your old life crumble; now create something in its place. It needn't be a big momentous project. In fact, putting pressure on yourself to make something significant and "productive" is often just an attempt to fix what was broken rather than creating something authentically new coming from you. I say start small and don't get stymied by needing it to "mean" anything. Create a garden, paint, dance, write, make a new group of friends, and create new experiences—anything that *feels* right. The intention is to demonstrate that you are not limited by the past but rather are a source of creation and a generator of newness, and you can chose to harness the flow whenever you need to reconnect with that power.

Stand Up When Necessary, But Pick Your Battles

As you go through your divorce—and especially if you need to continue interacting with your former partner as a co-parent—you will need to speak up. Only you know what you need and what you think is right for you. No one can do that for you. And if you let someone else choose, you will miss out on actively participating in the creation of your own future.

Standing up, however, does not mean being an immovable force in every decision. I suggest you pick your battles: confront when you need to but also freely give when it is possible. The act of giving can actually feel quite powerful. It can also model for your partner how flexibility can transform conflict and engender giving in your ex, as well. Saying, "Okay, I can live with that," feels incredibly awesome when it is done from a genuine place of letting go.

It also makes your firm stances more impactful. It signifies a true intention of standing firm rather than having it dismissed as an "emotional reaction." Aim for an assertive posture rather than an aggressive reaction. Assertive means communicating clearly that something is important: I'm listening and open, and while I am not going to try and push you, I will not be pushed back. Think of yourself standing tall with calm, relaxed shoulders and your body with a little sway but not lunging forward or shrinking backward.

This is what assertiveness feels like and the vision I create when I need to take a firm position. It helps me to find my center, manage my emotions, and form my words. Taking a clear and reasoned stance does wonders for your own sense of self, as well as helping you to distinguish between what is in your power and what is not.

Focus on What You Can Control

You can control many things: your behaviors, your thinking, and how you manage your own emotions. What you *cannot* do is control others. You can ask, explain, and negotiate, but ultimately they will do whatever they choose. You cannot make your ex think or feel as you do. If they are responsive and understanding, that is your great fortune. However, if they cannot be reasonable or responsive, there is not much you can do except continue to clarify your needs and communicate them with calm assertiveness.

You may have to accept differences or even a hostile ex who cannot or will not put down their anger or cease their attacks. If this is your lot, then maintain your own focus and find ways that you have power over a situation. If they try to bully you into accepting a decision you do not want, stay respectful but firm and say, "I understand, but no thank you." If they rage and attack, find some distance and create a safe space for yourself. If you have children, help them create a space of peace for themselves. Be their calm in the storm. Focus on you, not on your ex, and build the positive, peaceful life that is within your power to create.

Rewrite Your Story

As I've previously discussed, the story of what happened to you and your family creates the meaning of your experience. You will not only look back and see it written in your past but you can also use it to view the present and create your future. It should be authentic; it was and is a painful time, but see if you can find some goodness, something worth building a new life for you and your children.

Even if there are "bad actors," there might also be a hero. Or perhaps the "villain" is more nuanced. Decide for yourself which story you wish to live and the values you want it to convey. I believe hopeful, resilient, moving stories that build on our strengths and weave in our good and not-so-good experiences have a profound impact on how we and our children see our possibilities and ourselves in the future.

To explore your own story and the ways in which it may affect your children's process of making meaning, try the following exercise.

CHAPTER 18 EXERCISE: REWRITING YOUR STORY

Find some quiet space and think deeply about how you understand your divorce at this time. By deeply, I mean think about what happened, along with what you tell yourself and others about it: what it meant for you, what it means now, and what it might mean for your future. When you have a good idea, answer the following questions:

1. Are there any major themes in your story?
2. Who are the players and what are their roles?
3. How does this understanding shape your behaviors, thoughts, and beliefs about yourself?
4. How does this understanding influence your interactions with your ex?
5. Is this communicated to your children verbally or by nonverbal means, such as in your behaviors, attitudes, or interactions?

Take a moment to think about how your current story is helpful or not helpful:

1. Is there anything in your story, characters, or roles that you wish to maintain or strengthen? Change or alter?
2. How would doing so help as you move forward as an individual?
3. How might it help your children or family as a whole?
4. Are there any concrete steps you can take to either strengthen the good or mitigate the hurtful that you can commit to right now?

Epilogue

Full Transparency: What Helped Me

I don't wish to just wax philosophical, but I'm sure you want to know how I managed to make it thus far. I don't mind, as I think it only fair to share with you the ways in which I was lucky and blessed. I recognize it is not all about a can-do attitude, and I can give credit where credit is due. Several things were pivotal in supporting my family's good outcomes. This is not meant to be a list of requirements but rather an acknowledgement of what I found, in my own journey, to be good choices or fortunate happenings.

Collaborative Divorce

My former husband and I utilized collaborative law as our process for divorce. It is a nontraditional approach to divorce that uses interest-based negotiation rather than relying on litigation (or the threat of possible litigation). In all fairness, I had no prior knowledge of what kinds of divorce processes were available, much less collaborative ones. I might be wrong (I've never asked, but I'm sure he will correct me if I'm mistaken), but I believe my ex simply wanted to find the kinder, gentler way to end the marriage. I remember being a bit pissed that he had the audacity to try to "make it nice."

Since my modus operandi at that time was to do as little as possible to move the process forward, I found the closest collaborative law attorney and soon found myself in a room with both attorneys speaking in soothing tones about honesty, transparency, and durable agreements. For my part, I simply cried. Profusely, much to their discomfort. Still, as the process continued and my ex and I met with the divorce coaches (think marriage counseling but backward), I began to engage. I said all the things I felt needed to be said or just needed to hear myself say. Emotion was welcome, and we laid everything on the table while they slowly, steadily, began to create a framework for feeling and communicating our experience, while holding true to what we valued for our son and our individual futures.

It was not kinder and gentler, but it was honest; the team, true to their process, led us to speak about what we needed rather than what we could "get." They spoke to that reasonable, mature, honorable place that we forgot we had. I am convinced that this process was key to helping craft a settlement that allowed me to have his financial support so I could realize my need to raise our son as a stay-at-home mom for a few years before supporting my own household. As a mom to one, I am forever grateful.

It is important to note that I have no idea what kind of settlement would have emerged had we not gone through the collaborative process, but the important components for me were the experience of stating my needs and seeing my ex respond. It engendered a level of trust that we could each speak and be heard. We did not need the law to force us—the tether that held him to me and me to him was restrung.

I would be remiss if I did not mention my own independent strengths. I have a good education with a license to practice counseling that I could put to use post-divorce. My weakness, however, was that I have a family legacy of well-educated people with the motto of "Aim low." It was only the cold realities of divorce that forced me to challenge my fears and risk starting a private practice. I found support from where I never in my wildest dreams expected it, and I appreciate immensely their belief in me when I needed it and lacked self-confidence.

Lastly and most importantly, I discovered I had a decent and honest man as a partner in my divorce. Although he did not want to be married to me, he did show his capacity to listen, negotiate, understand, and give in ways that honored me as his son's mother and his former wife. What also helped is that I decided to stop looking backward and began looking to the present and the future. I stopped trying to punish him and focused on asking for what I needed. He, in turn, negotiated fairly and often understood what I needed even if he didn't agree. Even though his decision to divorce hurt me, I now know he took no pleasure in it. To this day we still have our disagreements, but the trust holds. The marriage may not have lasted, but in its place is the bond of mutual respect as people and as parents.

If you have many negative labels for your ex and feel hopeless that you can ever find a level of respect and trust, I would caution you not to give up hope. My experience as a clinician leads me to believe that while there are individuals incapable of behaving with goodwill and honesty, they are in the minority. But many couples give up without doing the hard work. It's often not about having both people possessing all of the needed components and a cooperative mind-set from the first step. It's about meeting the challenge ahead and growing into the people and parents who are required for the journey.

Suggested Resources

Feeling Better and Finding Inspiration

Action for Happiness: actionforhappiness.org

Mindsight: The New Science of Personal Transformation by Daniel J. Siegel

Rising Strong: How the Ability to Reset Transforms the Way We Live, Love, Parent, and Lead by Brené Brown

The Dance of Intimacy: A Woman's Guide to Courageous Acts of Change in Key Relationships by Harriet Lerner

The Happiness Project: Or, Why I Spent a Year Trying to Sing in the Morning, Clean My Closets, Fight Right, Read Aristotle, and Generally Have More Fun by Gretchen Rubin

Support for Children

A Smart Girl's Guide to Her Parents' Divorce: How to Land on Your Feet When Your World Turns Upside Down by Nancy Holyoke (ages 9–12)

Divorce is Not the End of the World: Zoe and Evan's Coping Guide for Kids by Zoe Stern and Evan Stern (ages 8–12)

How It Feels When Parents Divorce by Jill Krementz (ages 8+)

I Don't Want to Talk About It by Jeanie Franz Ransom (ages 4–8)

It's Not Your Fault, Koko Bear: A Read-Together Book for Parents and Young Children During Divorce by Vicky Lanski (ages 3–7)

Let's Talk About Divorce by Fred Rogers (ages 4–8)

Now What Do I Do?: A Guide to Help Teenagers With Their Parents' Separation or Divorce by Lynn Cassella-Kapusinski (ages 10–17)

The Boys and Girls Book About Divorce by Richard A. Gardner (ages 9+)

The Family Book by Todd Parr (ages 4–6)
Two Homes by Claire Masurel and Kady MacDonald Denton (ages 3–7)

Parenting in Separation or Divorce

Helping Children Cope with Divorce by Edward Teyber
Helping Your Kids Cope with Divorce the Sandcastles Way by M. Gary Neuman and Patricia Romanowski
Mom's House, Dad's House: Making Two Homes for Your Child by Isolina Ricci
Parenting After Divorce: Resolving Conflicts and Meeting Your Children's Needs by Philip M. Stahl
The Co-Parenting Handbook: Raising Well-Adjusted and Resilient Kids from Little Ones to Young Adults Through Divorce or Separation by Karen Bonnell and Kristin Little
The Parenting Plan Workbook: A Comprehensive Guide to Building a Strong, Child-Centered Parenting Plan by Karen Bonnell and Felicia Malsby Soleil
The Truth about Children and Divorce: Dealing with Emotions So You and Your Children Can Thrive by Robert Emery

General Parenting Support

1-2-3 Magic: Effective Discipline for Children 2–12 by Thomas W. Phelan
How to Talk So Kids Will Listen & Listen So Kids Will Talk by Adele Faber and Elaine Mazlish
Parenting from the Inside Out: How a Deeper Self-Understanding Can Help You Raise Children Who Thrive by Daniel Siegel and Mary Hartzell
Parenting with Love and Logic by Foster Cline and Jim Fay
Raising an Emotionally Intelligent Child: The Heart of Parenting by John Gottman, Joan DeClaire, and Daniel Goleman
Smart but Scattered Teens: The "Executive Skills" Program for Helping Teens Reach Their Potential by Richard Guare, Claire Dawson, and Colin Guare

Resolving Conflict Between Parents

A Guide to Divorce Mediation: How to Reach a Fair, Legal Settlement at a Fraction of the Cost by Gary J. Friedman

Divorce Without Court: A Guide to Mediation and Collaborative Divorce by Katherine E. Stoner

Getting to Yes: Negotiating Agreement Without Giving In by Roger Fisher and William Ury

The Good Divorce: Keeping Your Family Together When Your Marriage Comes Apart by Constance Ahrons

Finding Divorce Professionals and Legal Information Websites

Academy of Professional Family Mediators: apfmnet.org

American Bar Association: findlegalhelp.org

FindLaw: findlaw.com

International Academy of Collaborative Professionals: collaborativepractice.com

Reference Desk: refdesk.com/factlaw.html

Websites for Finding a Therapist and General Mental Health information

American Academy of Child & Adolescent Psychiatry: aacap.org

American Association for Marriage and Family Therapy: aamft.org

American Counseling Association: counseling.org

Mental Health/Immediate Help: mentalhealth.gov/get-help/immediate-help/index.html

PsychCentral: An Independent Mental Health Social Network: psychcentral.com

Acknowledgments

The Co-Parenting Handbook

I began writing *No More Us* about two years after my own divorce. I had no idea if or when it would ever become anything other than my own personal journal. Then, some time later, I was graciously asked by Karen Bonnell, a veritable giant in the Collaborative Law community, to share in writing her book, *The Co-Parenting Handbook.*

Writing with Karen helped me immensely in clarifying my thoughts on what helped children cope and families thrive in divorce. *The Co-Parenting Handbook* has allowed many to see what is possible in managing divorce without unnecessary suffering. However, I found I also wanted to tell the more intimate story of how to personally navigate the divorce process in a way that minimized pain and conflict.

In some ways, *No More Us* feels like a behind-the-scenes look at what it takes to move from grief and anguish to healing—and for divorcing parents, how to co-parent peacefully. I am grateful to have had the chance to work with Karen and am proud of *The Co-Parenting Handbook* for its support of families in their many forms, as well as for giving me the courage and confidence to share my own personal journey.

To my Collaborative family:

To Anne and Karen for being true superwomen and gracing me with your guidance. I am blessed to know you.

To Mark, Mike, John, Anne, and Tim for supporting our family through the darkest time, knowing the path, and relentlessly herding us when we strayed.

About the Author

Kristin Little, MS, MA, LMHC, is a licensed mental health counselor providing individual counseling for adults and adolescents, as well as family therapy to address child issues. She also serves as a collaborative child specialist for families during and after divorce. Kristin has twenty-three years' experience working with children and parents, supporting healthy development and effective and connected parenting. She is certified in Washington State as a child mental health specialist. In addition to child specialist and child-centered work, she also enjoys working with adults with anxiety, depression, body image issues, and difficult or challenging life transitions.

Kristin is an active member of Collaborative Professionals of Washington, a growing organization that is dedicated to reducing the harmful conflict of divorce for couples and families. She has experience as a community college instructor and is a frequent speaker for mental health and legal professional groups on the topic of healthy coping for parents and children in divorce. Kristin lives in the Northwest with a loving, large, and complicated two-home family.

Kristin Little has an active private practice in Kirkland, Washington, and can be reached at theevergreenclinic.com or through her website at kristinlittlecounseling.com.

Made in the USA
Monee, IL
01 March 2021